D1421407

HOW TO BE A POLITICIAN

2,000 Years of Good (and Bad) Advice

Leabharlanna Poiblí Chathair Baile Átha Cliath
Dublin City Public Libraries

VINCE CABLE

EBURY
PRESS

Ebury Press, an imprint of Ebury Publishing,
20 Vauxhall Bridge Road,
London SW1V 2SA

Ebury Press is part of the Penguin Random House group of companies
whose addresses can be found at global.penguinrandomhouse.com

Copyright © Vince Cable 2022

First published in the United Kingdom by Ebury Press in 2022

www.penguin.co.uk

A CIP catalogue record for this book is available from the British Library

ISBN 9781529149654

Text design by Jonathan Baker

Typeset in 11.5/16 pt Baskerville MT Std by Jouve (UK), Milton Keynes
Printed and bound in Great Britain by Clays Ltd, Elcograf S.p.A.

The authorised representative in the EEA is Penguin Random House Ireland,
Morrison Chambers, 32 Nassau Street, Dublin D02 YH68

Penguin Random House is committed to a sustainable future
for our business, our readers and our planet. This book is made
from Forest Stewardship Council® certified paper.

CONTENTS

INTRODUCTION

WHY, WHAT AND HOW

*'The desire to be a politician should bar you
for life from ever becoming one'*
Billy Connolly

*'There is no end to the praises that can
be sung of politics'*
Bernard Crick

WHY?

You want to be a politician. Really?

Your parents will think you are wasting a good education. Your friends will think you are weird. You wish to enter a 'profession' which is widely distrusted and disliked. Are you – seriously – up for that?

Perhaps you tell yourself that you want to go into politics because you 'want to make a difference' or you 'want to make the world a better place'. I suggest that you save that stuff for your speeches. Your heart may be in the right place, but it is more important to have your head screwed on the right way. In his essay 'Politics as a Vocation', written in Germany in 1919, Max Weber observed: **'Politics is made with the head, not with other parts of the body, nor the soul.'**

The ancients struggled to reconcile the ideals of democracy with the inescapable grubbiness of politics. Getting your hands dirty is a necessity, not a choice. As Pericles put it: **'Just because you do not take an interest in politics doesn't mean politics won't take an interest in you.'** Plato was more cynical: **'One of the penalties for refusing to participate in politics is that you end up being governed by your inferiors.'**

Even a modern saint like Gandhi was realistic about the political life: **'If I seem to take part in politics, it is only because politics encircles us today like the coil of a snake from which one cannot get out, no matter how much one tries. I wish therefore to wrestle with the snake.'**

I suggest, therefore, that you temper any idealised picture of the role of politicians that you may hold by listening to the public. They have a somewhat jaundiced view. Anyone living through recent British political history can understand why: the 'expenses scandal', which exposed many MPs as 'filling their boots' and manipulating expenses claims to inflate their income; repeated reports of sexual harassment and bullying; an ex-prime minister making a small fortune lobbying former colleagues on behalf of a questionable company; the disgrace of another prime minister flagrantly breaking lockdown rules he demanded the public obey. And on and on.

In fact, the low standing of politicians is near universal. The polling company Ipsos carried out a survey of 20,000 people in 23 countries for their views on the trustworthiness of 18 professions. From Brazil and Canada to India and Japan and to the UK and USA, politics was bottom of the league table almost everywhere.

It is too easy to say that the reputational damage was caused by a few 'bad apples'. There is a deeper problem. Other professions also have rogues and liars. Dr Shipman was a British doctor who murdered up to 250 of his patients and numerous others have been struck off for negligence or involved in hospital scandals involving many avoidable deaths, and yet medicine is invariably the most trusted and respected of professions. The police are still broadly respected, despite everything. Not so politicians.

If politicians are held in such low esteem, you might well ask why any rational individual would ever volunteer for endless ridicule and abuse. As George W Bush put it, with uncharacteristic insight, **'Everybody wants to be loved . . . You never heard anybody say, "I want to be despised, I'm running for office."'** One major reason is that people seem to make a distinction between politicians in general and politicians whom they know.

As a local MP, I used to brace myself for an evening of doorstep canvassing expecting a deluge of criticism, disillusionment and anger. I always came back glowing from the warmth of the reception, the compliments on my work and even the polite friendliness of known opponents. I persuaded myself that I had a particular talent – until other MPs told me that it was normal.

Some politicians inspire real affection and respect. The outpouring of genuine grief for the assassinated Jo Cox in 2016 was later matched by the deep feelings of goodwill towards David Amess. Other accolades are less understandable. I was recently travelling through the constituency of an MP who had announced his retirement. The headline in the local newspaper was: 'Dedicated MP Retires: our hard-working local champion'. Having seen him in action (or inaction) for a couple of decades, I was baffled that someone so hopeless should inspire such enthusiasm, but he did.

Some politicians inspire real warmth even before they retire or die. I accompanied Shirley Williams on political visits and saw her capacity to light up a room and to make everyone she met feel somehow special. It is said that Bill Clinton had a remarkable capacity for empathy in his dealings with people (even if it went from empathy to intimacy with some women). Others have been able to convey empathy on TV through their use of words or body language – for example, Tony Blair and Charles Kennedy.

You are entering a profession where you are disliked and distrusted in general but not necessarily in particular.

The distrust originates in the fact that politicians must win power to exercise it. Getting elected involves building a broad constituency of support which can easily be portrayed as 'trying to be all things to all people'. A US commentator observed that **'politics is getting votes from the poor and campaign contributions from the rich by promising to protect the one from the other'**.

To win power, you need to promise something to the voters. And yet it is very unlikely that all promises can be fully delivered, unless you have an exceptional gift for converting **'the poetry of campaigning into the prose of governing'**, to paraphrase former governor of New York Mario Cuomo. So, the public then feels let down. Obama's **'audacity of hope'** was unlikely to survive contact with reality (and it didn't). Churchill used honest realism to inspire his people with a vision of **'blood, sweat and tears'** but he wasn't – then – trying to win an election.

If you are a successful candidate for office, your political campaigning will raise people's hopes. Governing will then deflate them. It has been said that **'the only people bound by campaign pledges are the voters who believe them'** or, as Benjamin Disraeli put it: **'Politics, ill understood, has been defined as the art of governing mankind by deceiving them.'** Usually, politics is not quite so cynical. But for those whose hopes have been raised, a sense of betrayal and disillusionment can follow when, instead of delivering what they promised, the politicians for whom they voted embark on compromises with their opponents and critics.

I would say that compromise isn't a dirty word but a sign of grown-up politics. To achieve agreement requires cutting deals, horse-trading and arm-wrestling. It is often necessary to perfect the art of the possible and put practicality before ideology and undeliverable promises. Politics in a real democracy is all about managing conflict, differences of opinion and conflicting interests through political debate and engagement, rather than through violence and coercion. Nelson Mandela observed that, **'No problem is so deep that it cannot be overcome, given the will of all parties, through discussion and negotiation rather than force and violence.'**

As for the more mundane tasks of administration in functioning democracies, President Gerald Ford observed: **'Truth is the glue that holds governments together. Compromise is the oil that makes governments go.'**

So don't embark on a political career thinking of yourself as a knight in shining armour. It is a worthwhile and necessary job – like emptying the bins and keeping the sewers working: smelly and unglamorous, but vital.

WHAT?

So, you are still interested. We now need to be clearer as to what exactly you mean by being 'a politician', as they come in all kinds of shapes and sizes. Local and national. Full time and part time. You may quite likely mean a minister or MP, in Westminster. But the so-called 'Westminster bubble' doesn't define politics everywhere. If you live outside England you are much more likely to be familiar with Nicola Sturgeon or Michelle O'Neill and their colleagues, few of whom have served in Westminster or have any aspiration to do so. Increasingly, big English conurbations are led by politicians who have moved on – and up – from Westminster or bypassed it altogether: Andy Burnham in Manchester; Andy Street in the West Midlands; Tracy Brabin in West Yorkshire; Sadiq Khan in London. These are serious politicians.

And don't ignore local government, which can be entry-level politics or important in its own right. There are around 22,000 councillors in the UK representing wards in districts, counties, London boroughs and towns and cities. Most are paid, albeit not very handsomely, and a number are full-time politicians. Some have more power and influence, and more public recognition, than parliamentarians representing the same area. At the lowest level of government are parish councillors, who are unpaid and very part time but not to be ignored. Thanks to YouTube, Jackie Weaver of Handforth Parish Council has enjoyed more fame than many Cabinet ministers will ever do. It is also possible to enjoy a successful political career without winning an election. Nigel Farage could reasonably claim to have been the most consequential politician of his generation. Yet he stood seven times for Parliament for UKIP and lost, having earlier failed to be selected as a Conservative candidate.

The Farage story is illustrative of a wider point: that those who wish to pursue a political career through one of the smaller parties – UKIP and its various reincarnations; the Greens; the Women's Equality Party; various micro-parties of the extreme right or left – let alone as an independent, are most unlikely, under the British voting system, to reach Westminster. Even candidates of the third party, the Liberal Democrats, have the cards stacked against them (as I can testify from personal experience).

It is perfectly possible to become a successful and influential politician without ever troubling the voters at all. The House of Lords is now overwhelmingly appointed. Some of its members are figures of distinction with an enviable commitment to public service. Many are not. Some have done little more than make a donation to a political party or enjoy the patronage of a party leader. A peerage then entitles them to vote on and shape the laws of the land. They can even become a minister.

Then there are special advisers (SPADs) and press officers, sometimes called 'spin doctors' by the media. Some of these have acquired far more political power and influence, and fame, than elected politicians. Alastair Campbell, Tony Blair's spin doctor, remains a significant political figure, prolific on social media. Dominic Cummings, former adviser to Boris Johnson, was said, at one point, to be running the government (before he left and turned on his former boss). Then there are numerous other political figures, akin to mediaeval courtiers, jostling for influence: advisers, consultants, lobbyists, commentators. They may be current politicians, ex-politicians or future politicians, or people who are just politically powerful.

The good news is that there are lots of options. The bad news is that there isn't a recognisable pathway showing you where to go. That takes us to the 'How'.

HOW?

'Politics is the only profession for which no preparation is thought necessary'
Robert Louis Stevenson

You have decided that this is for you – hopefully without too many illusions. You have broadly decided what kind of political role you aspire to play: prime minister, backbench MP, mayor of Manchester, Sinn Féin councillor in Derry, an unelected baron, an advisory *éminence grise*.

Now you want to know how to go about it.

I wish I could recommend a suitable college or university course, apprenticeship, professional body or website. But there isn't one.

Despite having been one, I struggle to answer the question: 'How do I become a politician?' You will get one answer from a prodigy in their twenties who is tipped for the top. Another from the countless others of comparable talent who have spent a small fortune and a big chunk of their lives trying to get selected or elected but failed. And another from me; I got into Parliament at the fifth attempt, 30 years after I first tried with a different party (and then enjoyed 20 years in Parliament, 5 in the Cabinet). There are many roads into politics; most are winding, some lead nowhere, almost all are accident prone, a lot are impassable.

The answer to the question of how to get into politics has something to do with chance: managing to be lucky; engineering the good fortune to be in the right place, in the right party, at the right time.

There are also some character traits which help: resilience, stamina, patience, energy and a thick skin – qualities which are not easily taught. It is important to be able to communicate to a live audience, on TV, on radio, in print and on social media – though this you can learn. You also need to be able to work in a team whilst having a big enough ego to promote yourself.

These are generalisations. But politicians are very different in the way they see themselves and the job. I make a key distinction between priests and plumbers. Political priests campaign, preach, define values, create slogans, make speeches, write articles, argue the toss about policy and political ideas and hopefully inspire their flock with faith and hope. Obama was the perfect political priest; Jeremy Corbyn a less successful one.

The plumbers are interested in solving problems: getting things done, making things work, understanding the nuts and bolts, efficient organisation, teamwork. Isaiah Berlin saw political plumbing as the essence of the successful politician: **'What is it to be politically wise, or gifted, or even to be no more than politically competent, to know how to get things done?'** he wrote. The perfect plumber of modern times has been Angela Merkel, but she operated in a very different system of perpetual coalition government. President Lyndon B Johnson was a giant of political plumbing who achieved large-scale civil rights and social reform and was thoroughly unpleasant – and effective – with it. British politics has had a shortage of good plumbers.

I can't give you a road map to political success. I can tell you that a political career is challenging and unpredictable; often painful and difficult; quite likely to end in failure and frustration and possibly in humiliation. But, despite that, very worthwhile and necessary. As to how to navigate the treacherous waters, in each chapter that follows I'll end by collecting together the wise words of those who have gone before, starting at the beginning.

1

EARLY PROMISE

'He knows nothing and thinks he knows everything. That clearly points to a political career'
George Bernard Shaw, *Major Barbara*

EARLY ACHIEVERS

'Mothers all want their sons to grow up to be president, but they don't want them to become politicians in the process'
John F Kennedy

Since you have sought my advice on how to progress in a political career, I must be honest and tell you that it would have been better if you had been born into the right family. But it is too late for that. At the very least, you should get cracking as soon as you can. I speak as someone who entered Parliament aged 54 and didn't heed the advice of H A L Fisher, speaking to the young Richard Crossman: **'Go into Parliament while you are young. Whether you succeed or fail does not matter. It is the life which matters.'**

When a very young Boris Johnson announced his intention to be 'world king' and Harold Wilson set out to be prime minister, aged ten, their ambition was not misplaced. They reached the top (though not of the world).

No recent prime minister has, however, matched the youth of William Pitt the Younger, who achieved the position aged 24 and was subsequently regarded as one of the 'greats' for his leadership during the Napoleonic Wars with France (but in an era when only a privileged few were allowed to vote). The two closest are Tony Blair and David Cameron, both aged 43, which happens to also be the age of accession of the youngest American president (Kennedy).

Parliament once welcomed a 13-year-old MP, but that was in the seventeenth century. A recent prodigy is Mhairi Black, currently MP for Paisley, who was 20 when she entered as an SNP MP whilst still a Glasgow University student, the youngest MP since the 1832 Reform Act. Other 'Babies of the House', as the youngest members of the House are informally known, in recent years include two former leaders of the Liberal Democrats: Charles Kennedy and Jo Swinson. Going onto higher things, however, is not inevitable, as Michael Foot observed of one of his contemporaries: **'He passed** *from rising hope to elder statesman without any intervening period whatsoever.'*

POLITICAL DYNASTIES

*'Sometimes when I look at my children,
I say to myself: "Lillian, you should have
remained a virgin"'*
Lillian Gordy Carter, mother of Billy and Jimmy Carter

Achievers, be they early or late, make progress in politics through ambition, hard work and luck. Only a diminishing few have had the pure good fortune to be catapulted into politics by having the right genes: the hereditary privilege of automatic admission to the House of Lords. I guess you don't have blue or purple blood, or we wouldn't be having this conversation. In any event, the virtual extinction of hereditary peers has meant that the ballot box has replaced blood as a political qualification.

Dynasties have also been in retreat. The Churchills have been our leading political dynasty. But when Nicholas Soames departed the Commons in 2019, he was the last of the parliamentary Churchills: the second of two of Sir Winston's grandchildren, following Winston's son Randolph, his son-in-law Duncan Sandys (father of a Tory MP), Nicholas Soames's own father (another son-in-law of Winston) and the generations before, from Winston's father Randolph and others back to the eighteenth-century Duke of Marlborough. In 2019, a fourth generation Hurd MP also left (Nick, son of Douglas). There is still a fourth generation Benn (Hilary, son of Tony), a third generation Dunne (Philip) and quite a few second generation MPs: Lindsay Hoyle (the Speaker), Andrew Mitchell, Victoria Atkins, Bernard Jenkin, Ian Paisley Jnr and Stephen Kinnock. Other ancestors are more remote: Peter Mandelson is a grandson of Herbert Morrison and Labour's Harriet Harman has as her great-great-uncle, Joseph Chamberlain.

Dynastic politics also has a long tradition in the USA. The Bush family and its in-laws claim to go back to the eighteenth century and have produced two recent presidents. The Kennedy clan produced a president (JFK), two senators, Bobby and Teddy, and there have been fourth generation Kennedys in Congress. Despite President Clinton's support for his wife and Donald Trump's promotion of his daughter and son-in-law, dynasties, as in the UK, appear to be less fashionable than they were.

They remain popular in South Asia. India has produced four generations of Nehrus: Jawaharlal, Indira, Rajiv (all prime ministers) and Rahul, though the last of these and his Italian mother, Rajiv's widow, seem to have exhausted public enthusiasm for the family as leaders of Congress. Pakistan, Bangladesh and Myanmar all adopted, as prime minister, daughters of earlier leaders. Elsewhere, hereditary monarchs and hereditary dictators survive but not through the ballot box. Anyway, all of that is very far removed from the kind of political career you envisage.

EARLY YEARS AND BACK STORIES

'But then, he thought, most politicians are small and shabby, the sort of people who have been bullied at school. That's why they become politicians'

Anthony Horowitz, *Skeleton Key*

The politics of early years matters. You need to understand the backgrounds of your colleagues and rivals. Sometimes the story is predictable and boring: they inherited their parents' lifestyle, prejudices and party, and the discussions round the family dinner table, or the propaganda from the family newspaper, defined them for the rest of their lives. But usually there is more.

There is a key moment in a political career when you cease to be just an easily forgotten name, face and job and become a personality. A newspaper decides to run a feature on your life. This is your chance to set out your back story, the essential details of which then define you in the public mind. Try not to blow it. Theresa May's reputation never recovered from telling the world that the naughtiest thing she had ever done was to run through a field of wheat. She is an impressive figure of great integrity and some courage but the abiding image was of a rather prissy head girl.

For many politicians, the back story of their early years redeems them. Margaret Thatcher's image, with her upper-middle-class drawl and hectoring manner, was softened by the story of her humbler upbringing in Grantham and generous acknowledgement of the debt she owed to her father, Alderman Roberts the shopkeeper. She was easily recognisable as the nine-year-old who said, 'I wasn't lucky. I deserved it,' when she won a school prize and in the ICI personnel report describing the young Margaret Roberts as **'headstrong, obstinate and dangerously opinionated'**. But there was also her later reflection that, **'I just owe almost everything to my father and it's passionately interesting for me that the things that I learned in a small town, in a very modest home, are just the things that I believe have won the election.'**

Keir Starmer is often portrayed as a dull and worthy London lawyer but storytelling around his early life has brought out the fact that he is the son of a West Midlands metal worker and an NHS nurse whose political faith was sufficiently passionate to name their son after a socialist hero.

Some back stories are of struggles against disadvantage. Sajid Javid, the health secretary and former chancellor, is the son of an immigrant bus driver and got to the Cabinet through ambition and sheer hard work. Starmer's deputy, Angela Rayner, is recognisable on television for her auburn hair and broad, working-class Lancashire accent. She has become an iconic figure because of her background of poverty as the child carer of a mother with severe bipolar disorder, leaving school pregnant, aged 16, without qualifications and making her way through the trade union movement. Other leading Labour figures came alive for the public by over-coming childhood adversity: Alan Johnson was orphaned at 13, later became a postman and then general secretary of the postal workers' union; David Blunkett experienced childhood poverty after his father died in a horrific industrial accident and received little help for his blindness.

An engaging narrative doesn't need to be all about struggle and disadvantage. Boris Johnson's chaotic life-style, family life and indeterminate number of children represent endearingly human frailties to many of his supporters. One of the most recognised members of the government has been Jacob Rees-Mogg, thanks to his carefully cultivated image of an eighteenth-century 'young fogey' sitting unapologetically on a personal for-tune. In France, President Macron was able to overcome the disadvantage of being a rich and privileged Roths-child banker in part through the human-interest story of his apparently successful marriage to a woman more than 20 years his senior, in contrast to the usual French political tradition of powerful men with younger mistresses.

So, you need a back story and it needs to be authen-tic. Nothing is worse than a phoney history. Nobody knows where the story originated of Harold Wilson going to school in bare feet or at least together with chil-dren in bare feet due to extreme poverty, as background to a life of socialist struggle. His actual background was educated middle class and his father had been a Liberal activist who worked on one of Winston Churchill's

(Liberal) campaigns. Wilson was a major historical figure who won three elections for Labour but his honesty was always – perhaps unfairly – regarded as suspect. As MP and journalist Ivor Bulmer-Thomas put it: *'If he ever went to school without boots it was because he was too big for them.'*

EDUCATION, EDUCATION, EDUCATION

'We made our mistake when we sent him to college where he learnt to read'
Frances McGee, mother of Wyoming Democratic senator Gale McGee

It is probably a bit late to change this now but it would have helped you to have gone to the 'right' school. These provide networks of well-connected friends, which can be nurtured into adult life, and teachers who have the commitment, time and resources to organise debates or encourage the exploration of political ideas in the classroom. Of the 2019 intake of MPs, 29 per cent were from independent schools, compared to 7 per cent in the country at large. At Cabinet level, in 2020, the imbalance was even bigger: 65 per cent independent school, 27 per cent comprehensive.

Within this elite is a super-elite. One in ten of the private school MPs went to Eton, which claims to have produced nineteen prime ministers. David Cameron became head boy and Boris Johnson was prominent there. An Eton education, with its association of class privilege, has, however, not always been considered an asset, even in the Conservative Party. When Douglas Hurd was attacked for it, he observed: **'I thought I was running to be leader of the Tory party, not some demented Marxist outfit.'**

In any event, I would suggest that what matters is not which school but what you do there. For me, aged 16 and an inarticulate shy teenager, a crucial development was to be given the lead in the school play (*Macbeth*), teaching me a life skill: how to speak to a live audience without relying on cue cards and autocues. And don't look down on the 'rugger-buggers'; politics is about teamwork, not just individuals showing off their talent.

A big decision looming is 'which university'? The conveyer belt from top public school to Oxbridge to Parliament is no longer as predictable as it once was. But Oxbridge helps. Around 20 per cent of MPs and half the current Cabinet are Oxbridge graduates. It also matters what you do with your time there. A succession of politicians, especially Conservatives, learnt their debating skills in the Oxford Union whose ex-presidents include Michael Heseltine, William Hague, Boris Johnson, Michael Gove, Philip May (Theresa's husband), Alan Duncan, Damian Hinds, Mel Stride, Liz Truss and Sam Gyimah (later, Lib Dem). The Cambridge Union has also produced a long line of leading Conservatives: John Nott, Leon Brittan, Michael Howard, Christopher Tugendhat, Norman Fowler, Selwyn Gummer, Norman Lamont, Ken Clarke. (Also me, though at no time a Tory.)

You don't need to go to Oxbridge to learn how to debate. The Glasgow University debating union is arguably sharper, wittier and more brutal than its Oxbridge equivalents. It helped to launch the political careers of John Smith, Donald Dewar, Charles Kennedy, Menzies Campbell and Nicola Sturgeon. It is said that Charles Kennedy was the only student ever to win the Observer Mace competition twice.

In a political universe dominated by university graduates, you should think about the University of Life: a quality apprenticeship in industry or joining the armed forces. John Major struggled at school when his family were in turmoil, left at 15 with three O levels and trained to be a banker. He went on to become Conservative prime minister. Paddy Ashdown never sat A levels but served in the Royal Marines, then the Diplomatic Service and as a spy before plunging into Liberal politics via a period of unemployment, becoming leader of the Liberal Democrats. You could do worse. And Michelle Obama put it best when she said: *'Whether you come from a council estate or a country estate, your success will be determined by your own confidence and fortitude.'*

'He was born a politician.'
No, Ursula thought, he was born a baby,
like everyone else. And this is what he
has chosen to become.
Kate Atkinson, *Life After Life*

Intelligent – brilliant – resourceful. He spoils his
undoubted talents by his excessive assurance,
his contempt for other people's point of view and
his attitude of a king in exile.
War College report on Charles de Gaulle, aged 32

What do you want to be a sailor for? There are
greater storms in politics than you will ever find
at sea. Piracy, broadsides, blood on the decks.
You will find them all in politics.
David Lloyd George

Give us a child for eight years and it will be a
Bolshevik for ever.
Lenin (attrib.)

I had rather see any child of mine want
than he get his bread by voting in the House
of Commons.
Advice to his son William (father of Pitt the Elder) from
Thomas Pitt MP

Englishman, 25 years old, about five feet eight inches tall, indifferent build, walks with a forward stoop, pale appearance, reddish brown hair, small and hardly noticeable moustache, talks through his nose, and cannot pronounce the letter 's' properly.

Boer description of Winston Churchill after his escape from them

Bob, you dog, if you are not prime minister one day I shall disinherit you.

The challenge set by Sir Robert Peel's father, himself an MP

My choice early in life was either to be a piano player in a whorehouse or a politician. And to tell you the truth, there's hardly any difference.

Harry S Truman

Every politician should have been born an orphan and remain a bachelor.

Lady Bird Johnson

Blessed are the young, for they shall inherit the national debt.

Herbert Hoover

When I was a boy I was told that anybody could become president; I'm beginning to believe it.
Clarence Darrow

If your dreams do not scare you, they are not big enough.

Ellen Johnson Sirleaf

2

CHOOSING A SIDE

*'Sooner or later one has to take sides – if
one is to remain human'*
Graham Greene

If you were to tell me that you are undecided about
which party to support, I would have to say that it is fine
to be a floating voter but not to be a floating politician.
You must choose. To quote George H W Bush, **'It is no
exaggeration to say that the undecided could go one
way or the other.'** The way you go should ideally reflect
your convictions, if you have any.

This isn't like choosing a college or a car. It is almost
as important and definitive as choosing a life partner or,
even, a football club: Man City versus Man United; Cel-
tic versus Rangers. It is being part of a tribe. In general,
it is for life and must endure all political weathers: defeat
and relegation as well as victory. And as a politician your
job is not just to be a member but to lead and inspire the
supporters.

There is a limited choice of parties to join. In 200 years or so of British democracy, there have only been three serious parties; in the USA, two. They each have their long histories, myths and heroes.

If you are inclined to Labour, remember that behind what is now a party of middle-class graduates there is a heroic history of class struggle against injustice and inequality fuelled by anger, weakened only by internal schisms on grounds of ideology. Aneurin Bevan captured the tribal spirit: **'What is Toryism but organised spivery?'** and **'Nothing can eradicate from my heart a deep abiding hatred for the Tory party . . . as far as I am concerned, they are lower than vermin.'**

The Conservatives have the aura of power, having enjoyed it for most of the last two centuries and two thirds of the time since the Second World War. And it has its own tribal war cries, some of the more pungent of which coming from Margaret Thatcher: **'Trying to cure the British disease with socialism was like trying to cure leukaemia with leeches,'** or, **'They've got the usual socialist disease; they run out of other people's money.'** Others have tried to craft a more positive message, as with Boris Johnson: **'Voting Conservative will cause your wife to have bigger breasts and increase your chances of owning a BMW M3.'**

The hope of the middle way was expressed by Charles Kennedy for the Liberal Democrats: **'Labour is the music of Dire Straits; the Tories are the music of Simple Minds. But we are the New Kids on the Block.'**

In general and outside Scotland and Northern Ireland, politics is a good deal less polarised than in the United States. There, a majority of Republican and Democratic voters appear to regard the opposition as a threat to their way of life and believe that their own political tribe faces an existential threat. The choice of a British political party certainly isn't life-threatening and may not even be friendship-threatening. But you must choose.

MAKING UP YOUR MIND

'We all know what happens to people who stay in the middle of the road. They get run over'
Aneurin Bevan

It is make your mind up time. Some of your contemporaries have already made the jump, leaving you feeling either late or daunted – as Kurt Vonnegut put it, **'True terror is to wake up one morning and realise that your high school class is running the country.'** These 'hares' are following in the footsteps of politicians like William Hague and Jeremy Corbyn who were politically committed and active in their mid-teens and at least two recent prime ministers – Wilson and Johnson – had been eyeing the top job since primary school.

Most of us, however, are 'tortoises'. For example, I was interested in politics but struggled to make a choice of party. My father was (I thought) a very right-wing

Tory and we quarrelled badly about Suez and the empire when I was 13. My best friend was a communist and that lost its allure after the Hungarian uprising. I was looking for a middle way and opted for the Liberals. My teenage liking for the 'soft left' and the emerging European movement landed me on the big fault line in British politics. My views never changed fundamentally but left me having to zigzag from Liberal to Labour to SDP to Lib Dems.

I see that the foreign secretary Liz Truss also struggled to choose. She had 'very left-wing' parents but opted for the Liberal Democrats at university. She then migrated to the Tories.

Each generation has a trigger point for political activism and your choice may come down to how you think the political parties have positioned themselves on Brexit, the pandemic or climate change and zero carbon. Your choice of party may help anchor you there. As Benjamin Disraeli observed: **'Party is organised opinion.'**

A key factor in the choice of many young people is how the parties stack up when it comes to gender and ethnic equality. Despite producing two female prime ministers – one of whom (Thatcher) famously said, in 1973, **'I don't think there will ever be a woman Prime Minister in my lifetime'** – the Conservatives appear to be less welcoming to women (24 per cent of MPs versus 51 per cent for Labour), though the differential has narrowed. The biggest turnaround has been with the Lib Dems, who, in 1997, had only 3 women out of 46 and now have 10 out of 13. Ethnic minorities used to be drawn to the Labour Party, which campaigned for race equality and opened the parliamentary door to Black and Asian MPs. Now, after a campaign by David Cameron to bring ethnic minority candidates into 'safe' seats, there are 41 Labour, 22 Tory and 2 Lib Dem. And there are half a dozen senior ministers of African or Asian heritage.

CALCULATING THE ODDS

'Some men change their party for the sake of their principles; others their principles for the sake of their party'
Winston Churchill

Most politicians, as I have described, find their way into politics as a result of conviction or because of their background circumstances. But some are sufficiently cold-blooded to do a calculation as to which party will be the best vehicle for a political career. And even the idealistic and committed will have at the back of their minds the pros and cons of their choice. So it is not unreasonable for you to calculate the odds on making a success of a political career.

One calculation is how easy it is to get into Parliament through different party routes. One measure is the number of votes required to get elected. In 2019, it required 38,000 votes for every Conservative who got elected and 51,000 for every Labour MP, on average.

But, for smaller parties, the chances of getting elected are much reduced. It required 336,000 votes to elect a Liberal Democrat and 866,000 to elect a Green. This is because under the first-past-the-post system, representation is not proportional, and the system requires votes to be distributed 'efficiently' to 'winnable' and marginal seats. It is very unfair but until turkeys embrace Christmas it is unlikely to change soon. As Martin Bell observed, to get an independent elected, **'You need a good cause, a well-known candidate and a vulnerable incumbent.'** (And, he could have added, the backing of bigger parties.)

Self-interested individuals may nonetheless pursue a career with a smaller party if they judge that the system will change or because they believe that they can secure a nomination in a 'winnable' seat. One exception to the generalisation about small parties is that nationalists in Scotland and Wales, and Sinn Féin and the DUP in Northern Ireland, are even more 'efficient' than the Conservatives in England. But choice of a career with these parties is unlikely to be open to an aspirant English career politician sitting in London or Birmingham.

Another factor tipping the odds on choosing a traditional, big party is the greater likelihood of a period in government. In the post-war era, Conservatives have spent 48 years in government, Labour 27 and the Lib Dems 5. A period in government increases the chance of being a minister, with the prestige and financial rewards attached, and the chance of a post-parliamentary peerage and other perks.

But the past isn't necessarily a guide to the future. A political career could last 50 years. Someone making a self-interested calculation in 1900 would probably have opted for the Liberals; in 2000 for Labour. Things change.

COMMITMENT

Once you make your choice, it is likely to be permanent. There are occasional defections – more in local than national politics. They are usually noteworthy and controversial but of no lasting significance. There is one major exception: Churchill.

Churchill was not merely a famous defector but a double defector, for which he was unapologetic: **'Anyone can rat; it takes a certain ingenuity to re-rat.'** He was initially elected as a Conservative but left for the Liberals shortly after, asserting, **'I am an English Liberal. I hate the Tory party, their men, their words, and their methods.'** He served in successive Liberal Cabinets, then returned to the Conservatives 20 years later. It is not a coincidence that his return overlapped with the decline and disintegration of the Liberal Party, after a century of electoral dominance, alternating in power with the Tories, and its replacement by Labour for most of the last century.

In the post-war era, there have been two major schisms. The first was when, in 1981, the 'Gang of Four' led a breakaway from Labour: totalling 28 Labour MPs (and 1 Tory). The newly formed SDP failed to break the two-party mould but by merging with the Liberal Party became the Liberal Democrats. The second was the split over Brexit, which led to a dozen Conservatives and several Labour MPs leaving their party.

One big lesson is that new parties do not survive in Britain's first-past-the-post electoral system. Most recently, the Change UK Party survived only a few months. Those entering politics often want 'something new'. In fact, the choice is very limited and largely restricted to something old. Don't be tempted.

THE NEXT STEPS

You have made your choice. What to do next? Parties tend to be suspicious of newcomers announcing that they are interested in a political career. My advice is to show that you are serious by throwing yourself into the hard graft of politics: get involved with the local party delivering leaflets, knocking on doors, stuffing envelopes and volunteering to sit freezing outside polling stations on election day. Travel to by-elections and put in a decent shift, even if the cause is hopeless. Show that you have political potential by offering to stand for the council in a ward where the party has no organisation, build up a team, get out leaflets and do serious canvassing. And, ideally, win. You need to learn to suppress yawns at party meetings where there is endless procedural wrangling; anguished debate over motions demanding that the government or the United Nations take note of the concerns

of the Little Tuddlebury branch of the party and inter-
minable argument around the detailed arrangements for
the next fundraising event.

If you discover that politics is your natural habitat there
is a route into the profession by becoming, in effect, a professional politician. Get a job as a researcher for an MP,
learning how the system works, picking up gossip on opportunities for new candidates and building up a network of
contacts. Alternatively, become a professional campaign
manager for the party, organising activity for local and
national elections. Or get elected for a significant local council, especially in one of the big cities, and make a mark there.
You may get the chance to be a special adviser to a senior
Cabinet minister, which puts you at the centre of power.

A third of Tory MPs and half of Labour MPs came
into Parliament in this way (with the smaller parties at a
similar level). Prominent Tories like David Cameron and
George Osborne both worked in Conservative Central
Office, with David Cameron being a special adviser to
the chancellor (Norman Lamont); the two Milibands
and Ed Balls also had party or policy advisory roles for
Labour. Some deplore the emergence of a class of 'professional politicians' who have limited experience of the
'real world' outside politics. But it has become a good
way into top-level politics and you have the advantage of
knowing how Parliament and government work before
you get there. But getting there isn't straightforward.
And as the following words attest, even once you're there,
you'll still have a lot to think about.

The first duty of a man is to think for himself.
José Martí

*Of the three parties I find Labour least painful.
My objection to the Tories is temperamental,
and my objection to the Liberals is Lloyd George.*
Bertrand Russell

*By far the most radical man I've known in
politics ... If it hadn't been for the war he'd have
joined the Labour Party. If that had happened
Macmillan would have been prime minister,
and not me.*
Clement Attlee on Harold Macmillan

If a man hasn't discovered something that he will die for, he isn't fit to live.

Martin Luther King

A faith is something you die for. A doctrine is something you kill for. There is all the difference in the world.

Tony Benn

It is often easier to fight for one's principles than it is to live up to them.

Adlai Stevenson

That's the difference between our two parties. Labour's still fumbling with its flies while the Tories are enjoying a post-coital cigarette after withdrawing our massive Johnson.

Ruth Davidson

Conservatism discards Prescription, shrinks from Principle, disavows Progress; having rejected all respect for antiquity, it offers no redress for the present, and makes no preparation for the future.

Benjamin Disraeli, *Coningsby*

An absolute monarchy tempered by regicide.

William Hague on the Conservative Party

If I could not go to Heaven but with a party, I would not go there at all.

Thomas Jefferson

I belong to no organised party. I am a Democrat.
Will Rogers

A *free society* is *a society where it* is *safe to be* unpopular.

Adlai Stevenson

A party of order or stability, and a party of progress or reform, are both necessary elements of a healthy state of political life.
John Stuart Mill

If there are two parties a man ought to adhere to that which he disliketh least, though in the whole he doth not approve it; for whilst he doth not list himself in one or the other party, he is looked upon as such a straggler that he is fallen upon by both.
George Savile, 1st Marquess of Halifax

Nothing but a load of kippers – two-faced, with no guts.
Eric Heffer on the Conservatives

I am sure that the party system is right and necessary. All cannot be fly-halves; there must be a scrum.

A P Herbert

Homophobic, racist, misogynistic . . . scum.

Angela Rayner on the Conservatives

On the road to Socialism, the Conservative Party has, in the past, been an accessory after the fact.

Sir Keith Joseph

Growing older, I have lost the need to be political, which means in this country the need to be Left. I am driven into the grudging toleration of the Conservative Party because it is the party of non-politics, of resistance to politics.

Kingsley Amis

All political parties die at last of swallowing their own lies.

John Arbuthnot, eighteenth-century Scottish physician

There is nothing to be got by being a Liberal today. It is not a profitable or a remunerative career.

Herbert Asquith, 1920

When a nation's young men are conservative, its funeral bell is already rung.

Henry Ward Beecher

Liberalism is the trust of the people tempered by prudence; Conservatism is distrust of the people tempered by fear.

William Gladstone

Vote Labour and you build castles in the air. Vote Conservative and you can live in them.

David Frost on *That Was the Week That Was*, suggested election slogan

---

We are the trade union for the nation as a whole.

Edward Heath on the Conservative Party

I think I am guilty of no absurdity in calling myself an advanced conservative liberal.

Anthony Trollope

There is no Democratic or Republican way of cleaning the streets.

New York City mayor Fiorello La Guardia

A circular firing squad.

Jeffrey Archer on the Conservative Party under John Major

Morris Udall had said:
When the Democratic Party forms a firing squad, we form a circle.

The Democrats are in a real bind. They won't get elected unless things get worse, and things won't get worse until they get elected.
Jeane Kirkpatrick

Like a stage coach. If you rattle along at great speed everybody inside is too exhilarated or too seasick to cause any trouble. But if you stop, everybody gets out and argues about where to go next.
Harold Wilson on the Labour Party

The day the SNP's problems began was the day it recruited its second member.
Fergus Ewing

The Liberals are the flying saucers of politics. No one can make head nor tail of them, and they never are seen twice in the same place.
John Diefenbaker

I'm not very keen for doves or hawks. I think we need more owls.
George Aiken

The Republicans are thinking of changing the Republican Party emblem from an elephant to a condom, because it stands for inflation, halts production, and gives a false sense of security while one is being screwed.

Joseph Rosenberger

Future generations are not going to ask us what political party were you in. They are going to ask what did you do about it, when you knew the glaciers were melting.

Martin Sheen

3

RUNNING FOR OFFICE

'We'd all like to vote for the best man,
but he's never a candidate'
Kin Hubbard

'The best argument against democracy is a five-
minute conversation with the average voter'
Winston Churchill

You have taken the first steps in a political career: joined a party; gained a bit of experience as an activist. You are beginning to understand how your chosen party works. You now want to take the plunge and stand for Parliament in a 'winnable' seat.

Running for political office is to take a step into the unknown. That is also true of many of the big decisions of life: marriage; starting a business; moving house. But in politics, the obstacle course is particularly long and arduous. John Major was right when he said, **'The first** *requirement in politics is not intellect or stamina but patience. Politics is a very long-run game and the tortoise will usually beat the hare.'* It's a long slog and the process of selection, the uncertain and taxing period of campaigning and the election itself all have hazards. The first hazard is that difficult conversation you must have with a partner and, perhaps, children explaining what is in store. It will be a tricky conversation.

SPELLING OUT THE COSTS

'It is now known . . . that men enter politics solely as a result of being unhappily married'
Cyril Northcote Parkinson

'Obviously [my daughters] – and Michelle – have made a lot of sacrifices on behalf of my cockamamie ideas, the running for office and things'
Barack Obama

As a prospective politician, you live with chronic uncertainty. Although the Cameron–Clegg coalition government tried to establish more predictability through the Fixed-term Parliaments Act, the experiment was brief. The system has reverted to the traditional format whereby you can be summoned to the campaign trail with as little as three weeks' notice. An election can be called when you are ill, giving birth, on holiday on the other side of the world, moving house or in a work crisis. And you are expected to be there when your helpers are out on the streets campaigning for you.

For seats which are 'marginal', the outcome is in doubt, and in elections such as those in 1997, 2015 and 2019 the definition of marginal was very broad. There are many tales of candidates in 'hopeless' seats in local or national elections who ran out of a sense of duty to keep their party on the ballot paper, as a 'paper candidate', or to gain experience, and found themselves elected. Conversely, there are those who planned their lives around a winning a 'safe' seat and lost.

Even when the timing of the election and the outcome are predictable, there are real costs involved in running for office. Candidates in 'winnable' seats, where the prospects can be inflated by wild optimism in a local or national party, will be expected to campaign and get themselves known for a period of what can be years. If you are local, you may be expected to devote your life to campaigning. If you are not local, you may be pressed by the local or national party to demonstrate seriousness by going to live in the constituency – or, at the very least, acquire a house there. And where does that leave your partner who also has a job or your children who are attached to their local school? You may be letting yourself in for a big bill in income forgone, relocation costs, careers interrupted and travel; estimates are of over £100,000 for some recent – unsuccessful – candidates. And that is ignoring the wear and tear on relationships, the time not spent with loved ones. Thirty years ago, I came close to being deselected as the candidate in

Twickenham when I was seen by the activists as giving too much attention to my family and my demanding job in a multinational company. I survived through luck and a few good friends.

If, after all that, you get elected you are, initially at least, on the salary and employment conditions of a backbencher. At present, the salary is close to £82,000. For many people, that is a small fortune. It is well over twice the median salary for full-time workers (£31,000) and over four times the annual equivalent of the minimum wage. But for highly paid professionals, senior managers and successful businesspeople, it is a fraction of the sum they would expect outside politics.

Politics has long been better remunerated in the USA but this hasn't muted dissatisfaction; as Harry S Truman griped, **'The difficulty with businessmen entering politics, after they've had a successful business career, is that they want to start at the top.'** Rather earlier, John Adams confessed to his wife, Abigail, in 1770, **'I have accepted a seat in the House of Representatives, and thereby have consented to my own ruin, to your ruin, and to the ruin of our children.'**

For those of today's MPs foolish or arrogant enough to complain publicly that pay is too low, there is the certainty of ridicule, a mauling in the popular press and invitations to visit the local food bank. If you feel impoverished, you may be tempted to take on second jobs but that has become hazardous politically, especially if it involves activities like lobbying or gives the impression that being an MP is the second job. Don't.

MPs are reluctant to be seen voting for their own pay increases but are equally reluctant to accept independent pay awards which are seen as too generous. MPs have also been obliged to curb very generous, non-contributory pensions. So, in relative terms, MPs have gradually fallen behind other prestigious occupations. There are allowances for staff, in Parliament and in the constituency; extra living expenses for MPs representing constituencies outside the home counties and travel. Misuse of these expenses, however, caused a major scandal in 2008/9 and there are continued rumblings of public discontent over such practices as hiring relatives. The fierce competition to be candidates in 'safe' or 'winnable' seats does not, however, suggest that the general slide in relative pay and conditions has deterred applicants from becoming MPs.

GETTING SELECTED

'Politics is show-business for ugly people'
Paul Begala

'The party needs a candidate who, positively, will make the widest appeal and, negatively, will offend the least proportion of the electorate'
Harold Laski

In theory, anyone can stand for Parliament who has £500 to burn and is not in prison serving a sentence over a year in length. Most ballot papers will have a list of names from small parties and eccentric one-man bands. My recent opponents included a man demanding a return to the fundamentals of the Magna Carta, various schismatic Christians, a proponent of levitation, a Republican and a breakaway Liberal. It is almost as hopeless to be a Conservative in Hackney, Labour in Esher or a Liberal Democrat in Lanarkshire. Candidacy in such places usually shows dedication to the cause, a willingness to serve an apprenticeship or wildly inflated optimism.

For serious parties, there is, however, the process of becoming an approved candidate. Even for 'hopeless' seats, parties will want to ensure that they have credible standard-bearers. A lot of damage can be done by candidates who have used social media to fire off homophobic or racist tweets; have had lurid, publicised sex lives; have run dodgy businesses; or defect a few days before polling. The process of interviewing and approval can be expensive and very time-consuming. I recall that my Lib Dem candidacy (in the days when our public support was too low to be measured in the polls) was stalled for over a year after one member of a national panel took exception to the style of a draft press release that I had written.

If you get onto the panel of approved candidates there then follows the selection process at constituency level. For a 'winnable' seat this can be ferociously competitive and demanding. The first step is to get onto a shortlist, which can involve getting access to key officials, like the constituency chair and executive officers, nods

and winks from head office and competition to win nom-
inations at branch level (or from trade unions in the case
of the Labour Party). If competition is tough, serious
candidates will then expect to produce glossy leaflets and
CVs for distribution to all the party members in the area
and to indulge in telephone canvassing or, even, doorstep
canvassing of members. Your CVs will be padded out
with reference to conferences attended and by-elections
campaigned in, and party bigwigs whose names can
plausibly be dropped. For the selectorate, there is an
opportunity to judge just how eager, or desperate, as well
as how able you are. If you come across as a hungry candidate, it is assumed that you will have a big appetite for
campaigning (and perhaps putting in money).

The crescendo of the selection process will usually be
a public meeting of all the members to hear the applicants speak and answer questions. For a lively local party,
this could involve a meeting of hundreds. But it could
equally involve a dusty room with a handful of disen-
gaged activists. The Labour Party selection process
involves delegates from local and union branches who
may be mandated to support favoured candidates. I
recall, during my days in the Labour Party in Glasgow,
where I was a city councillor, walking home from a selection conference for a 'safe' seat with the future first
minister of Scotland (Donald Dewar) trying to puzzle
out why our popularity, eloquence and careful planning
had produced only three votes between the two of us.
The trade union nominee had secured a comfortable
majority before opening his mouth.

These selection meetings can be dramatic occasions. After my own difficulties three decades ago with the local Lib Dem Party in Twickenham, I faced a re-selection against two of the party's rising stars who were thought likely to put in more effort than the labouring incumbent candidate (me). In a mass meeting of hundreds of members, I scraped through by a couple of votes after my supporters had mobilised a minibus to bring in a group of very elderly ladies and an even older retired bishop. Had I lost I would have disappeared into political obscurity.

Dramatic or otherwise, the traditional selection process has two big drawbacks. The first is that candidates appeal to party activists rather than the wider public. The Conservatives sought to counter this by holding some American-style primaries. Such a system produced outstanding candidates grounded in the real world (like Sarah Wollaston and Heidi Allen) but who were too independent-minded and rebelled, eventually leaving the party (over Brexit). The experiment has been quietly dropped.

The second problem is 'unconscious bias' against women and Black and Asian candidates. There are numerous horror stories of female applicants being accused of abandoning the needs of their spouses and children, and ethnic minority candidates being told that 'they are not a good fit' in white, rural and suburban seats. Labour and Lib Dems have used all-women short-lists with considerable success, but Labour found that when the restriction was lifted men were overwhelmingly chosen, again. David Cameron intervened forcefully to insist on 'safe' Conservative seats adopting more ethnic minority candidates, which they have done, with none of the predicted loss of 'white' votes, resulting in an influx of talented and ambitious future ministers.

ELECTION

'Promises, and pie crusts, are meant to be broken'
Jonathan Swift

There is then the business of getting elected. In practice, the outcome of elections is decided largely by the national campaign and often in the few days before voting. But for you, the candidate, there are years of hard slog 'working the constituency', building up name recognition, identifying and meeting the few hundred voters who might make the difference in a close count. Determined candidates can devote a decade or more of their lives to fighting several elections in the same seat, building up a 'personal vote'. The real reason for the long slog is to build up a local machine.

A lot of budding politicians, especially those who had a helping hand from head office and were 'parachuted' in to secure a nomination, get a very rude shock when they encounter the local party machine. If you are very lucky, you will find premises, a full-time organiser, motivated helpers and a healthy bank balance topped up by a big membership or a local grandee or a trade union.

For every such political Ferrari, however, there are dozens of Mondeos and very often an ancient banger a long way from roadworthy.

As the new 'prospective candidate', you must first assemble a team: someone smart and well-organised to prepare, cost and oversee the plan of action; someone who can help identify and organise the volunteers who are needed for campaigning; someone who can repair the broken IT system and sort out piles of ancient data; someone who can help fundraise to pay for a professional organiser and other basics; someone who can help defuse the personality conflicts which rage in many local parties and get onside the angry, jealous locals who were passed over in the selection. Team building, especially of volunteers, is an art and most budding politicians, who are temperamentally egotistical, either don't know where to start or think they can do everything themselves and burn out quickly.

Money matters. Joe Biden hit the nail on the head when he described politics as **'a damned expensive business; I had one hell of a time trying to raise money as a candidate'**. British parliamentary elections specify a small, strictly enforced spending limit – currently around £12,000 for an average constituency – for the three or four weeks of the campaign for which the election agent is legally responsible. The spending limit gives the entirely false impression that political campaigning is cheap. A competitive campaign over, say, a couple of years will cost well into six figures, taking in the expense of printing, premises and some paid staff. The candidate may have naïvely believed that the constituency would be in line for a share of the money donated to the party by Russian oligarchs or given as a down payment for a peerage (or, if Labour, from a big union). Then the truth gradually dawns that this money is disappearing in head office salaries and national advertising. If there is a bit of money left over it has more conditions than an IMF loan. Operation Bootstraps.

You may be lucky. There may be a friendly local billionaire who will sign cheques, or an ace fundraiser. But the candidate will be expected to lead from the front, bidding enthusiastically in the auction at the fundraising dinners – acquiring family holidays at the chairman's villa in the South of France when the family was planning to go camping in the Highlands of Scotland; building up a cellar of obscure liqueurs which have done the round of numerous tombolas; acquiring enough second-hand books to start a bookshop. Any residual shyness will be expunged by the necessary task of begging hard-up supporters for money. You may eventually acquire the skills which enable you to echo John F Kennedy at a fundraiser: **'I am deeply touched – but not as deeply touched as you have been in coming to this dinner.'**

Your campaign team wants to get you in front of the voters in humble, listening mode. Charles de Gaulle claimed that, **'In order to become the master, the politician poses as the servant.'** For an aspiring British politician today, this means manning street stalls, pushing unwanted leaflets into the hands of harassed shoppers and lots of canvassing. Some people genuinely like to see politicians in the flesh on their doorstep and want to engage in political chat. But an unknown individual wearing a rosette, asking how you plan to vote at the next election, is less likely to get a smile and an answer. The visit may be highly unwelcome if it wakes the baby, sets the dogs barking or interrupts *Coronation Street* or a crucial football match. I recall a naked lady who was deeply distressed to discover that I wasn't the expected milkman.

You must also take care that you are not following in the footsteps of canvassers from another party, or Jehovah's Witnesses, or the needy young man selling brushes on commission, working the same street and building up a climate of irritation. And unless the canvassing candidate is experienced in interpreting voters' body language, they will come back with wildly inaccurate data on voting intentions. Remember, too, that you can never please all these people: as Robert Kennedy astutely observed, **'One fifth of the people are against everything, all the time.'**

You may have set out on your political journey thinking that you are there to solve the world's problems. You will soon discover that your passionately held views are of little relevance to campaigning. Rather, you are on a crash course to developing skills as a doorstep and telephone salesperson, IT first-aider, fundraiser, diplomat, postperson, photographer, graphic designer, psychotherapist, accountant and auctioneer. And the advice from your campaign team and head office will be that your most useful contribution will be to keep out of trouble and avoid bad publicity. If you are up on a drink-driving charge, you will not get much sympathy for telling the judge, like the (unsuccessful) candidate Derek Laud: *'I can't take my chauffeur everywhere.'*

Once the election proper arrives you may have an opportunity to debate the issues with candidates from other parties and in the local press (if there is one; many have disappeared). Hustings meetings will be organised by local churches and charities. Unfortunately, the incumbent MP may not deign to turn up. The stage may be dominated by fringe candidates who have paid a deposit for the privilege of being a candidate and intend to enjoy their moment in the sun. In the unlikely event of a serious debate between serious candidates, the audience will be overwhelmingly made up of people who have already made up their mind and have come to cheer their champion. Not a vote will have been won.

So, please don't complain that I didn't warn you. I'll now hand over to others to add their own wisdom and their warnings . . .

Now and then an innocent man is sent to the legislature.
Kin Hubbard

We do not have government by the majority. We have government by the majority who participate.
Thomas Jefferson

The reason there are so few women politicians is that it is too much trouble to put make-up on two faces.
Maureen Murphy

The human brain starts working the moment you are born, and never stops until you stand up to speak in public.
George Jessel

It is not in the nature of politics that the best men should be elected. The best men do not want to govern their fellow men.
George MacDonald

The Republicans have a 'me too' candidate running on a 'yes but' platform, advised by a 'has been' staff.
Adlai Stevenson

Democracy is being allowed to vote for the candidate you dislike least.

Robert Byrne

The kind of politician who would cut down a redwood tree, and then mount the stump and make a speech on conservation.

Adlai Stevenson on Richard Nixon

One thing I resent is the slur that I just support political candidates because of the business.

Rupert Murdoch

You call my candidate a horse thief, and I call yours a lunatic, and we both of us know it's just till election day. It's an American custom, like eating corn on the cob. And, afterwards, we settle down quite peaceably and agree we've got a pretty good country – until [the] next election.

Stephen Vincent Benét

If you really want to diminish a candidate, depict him as the foil of his handler.

Karl Rove

During a political campaign everyone is concerned with what a candidate will do on this or that question if he is elected except the candidate; he's too busy wondering what he'll do if he isn't elected.

Everett Dirksen

Show me a good loser, and I'll show you a loser.

Henry Kissinger (attrib.)

Democracy is a form of government that substitutes election by the incompetent many for appointment by the corrupt few.

George Bernard Shaw

Some of the electorate might feel they have no choice: it's either Cocks or Dicks.

Labour chief whip Michael Cocks, on being challenged at Bristol South by the Conservative Terry Dicks

There's a lot of bleeding idiots in this country, and they deserve some representation.

Labour MP Bill Stones

Voting is merely a handy device; it is not to be identified with democracy, which is a mental and moral relation of man to man.

G D H Cole

Your representative owes you, not his industry only, but his judgment; and he betrays, instead of serving you, if he sacrifices it to your opinion.

Edmund Burke, to the electors of Bristol

Aye, lad, but never forget – Monty had a picture of Rommel in his bloody caravan.

Retort from an engineering worker to Winston Spencer-Churchill after he spotted his photo on the man's machine during the 1967 Gorton by-election

---

Never give your political opponent an audience he cannot attract by himself.

Harold Macmillan

I well remember my first campaign. My opponent called me a cream puff . . . Well, I rushed out and got the bakers' union to endorse me.

Claiborne Pell

If your opponent is drowning, throw the SOB an anvil.

James Carville

In England, of course, we stand for election; in more dynamic America, they run.

Hugh Brogan

Never trust a man when he's in love, drunk or running for office.

Shirley MacLaine

Politicians live in little worlds of their own and imagine that they are the universe.

Michael Foot

Popularity should be no scale for the election of politicians. If it would depend on popularity, Donald Duck and the Muppets would have seats in the Senate.

Orson Welles

Elections belong to the people. It's their decision. If they decide to turn their back on the fire and burn their behinds, then they will just have to sit on their blisters.

Abraham Lincoln

The English think they are free. They are free only during the election of members of Parliament.

Jean-Jacques Rousseau

4

GETTING STARTED

'Thank heaven Election Day is over.
No more campaign ads, no more mud-slinging,
no more candidates pretending they're straight.
It's over!'
Craig Ferguson

You are one of the successes of the night. You have finally made it. All those months or years of campaigning, the rows at home over absenteeism and the nerve-shredding arguments in the local party are behind you. At least, until the next election when you must defend the seat.

Speaker Bernard Weatherill commented, after the 1987 election, **'A number of people got in by mistake at the last election.'** You may well feel like one of them, at least at first. You start your parliamentary career in a state of mental and physical exhaustion. You missed a night's sleep when the votes were counted – and, perhaps, recounted* – followed by a round of speeches thanking the election officials, police officers, the other candidates, party helpers and all the countless sources of political inspiration and sacrifice who got you there.

Dazed and semi-conscious, and sustained by adrenalin, you head off the following day to Parliament, there to meet your new colleagues, pausing for a group photograph with the Great Helmsman who has steered the party through the election. Popping down on the Tube from Hackney or Richmond is, of course, different from what is to become a weekly journey from Cornwall or Orkney and Shetland. The first conversations with colleagues will be a lesson in British political geography and will remind you that being an MP can mean very different things in different places as well as in different parties.

FIRST STEPS

As a new boy/girl you are at the bottom of a hierarchy below returning MPs, particularly the stars who won high-profile battleground seats, and the irritating group of new MPs who seem to already know how everything works – former researchers to MPs and political advisers. There is no training and everyone else is lost,

---

* Not to rub it in, but you'd have been wise to listen to Benjamin Harrison: **'I knew that my staying up would not change the election result if I were defeated, while if elected I had a hard day ahead of me. So I thought a night's rest was best in any event.'**

having no idea what the job entails. In what the old-timers regard as 'the good old days' there was little to alleviate the confusion and newly minted MPs were largely left alone to work out how to navigate the myriad of corridors, get paid and follow the weird rituals. Now, there are helpful officials with welcome packs and induction interviews but, still, the newness can be overwhelming.

An early task is finding an office: somewhere to park your backside. The party whips control the allocation process and you will quickly learn that these are not people to cross. If they like you, you may get a room in Portcullis House with a modern office and space for staff. It is one of the most expensive public buildings in the country and is a masterpiece of neo-Gothic architecture, twenty-first-century advanced engineering and mediaeval plumbing with occasionally flushing loos. If, however, you are offered what looks like a broom cupboard you know you are off to a bad start.

Then there are staff. Most MPs have little knowledge of employment law, professional recruitment or staff management but, very quickly, must hire a team of people both in the constituency and in Parliament. A bad choice can lead to the MP having a reputation for incompetence: not answering letters, missing appointments and failing to respond to press enquiries. Or it can lead to employment tribunals, staff complaints and personality clashes in the office. These are problems experienced by many organisations but, for an MP, these dramas are often played out in the public eye and amplified by local gossip.

You will need an efficient, tactful, financially literate constituency office manager and a diary secretary; a knowledgeable and empathetic person to handle personal casework; someone to handle the press; someone to keep oiled and serviced the local political machine; someone to help with all the research required to be prepared for parliamentary work. And they must get on. It can take years to get the right people and the right chemistry. Whilst it happens, you must sort out priorities, deciding how to manage time amongst the numerous competing demands.

PRIORITIES: THE CONSTITUENCY

You can spend a great deal of time rushing from one committee or event to another and, despite having a full diary and constant exhaustion, achieve little. Priority setting is essential. There are five roles which are overlapping but represent different priorities: constituency work; campaigning; scrutiny; legislating and aiming for ministerial office (or a leadership role in opposition).

What constitutes a 'good constituency MP' is subjective and has changed over time. The political greats of the past, or even the not-so-greats, would never have rushed back to their constituencies every weekend. A monthly, or even three-monthly, visit would suffice. Now, only those MPs with very 'safe' seats can afford to be so cavalier. For the nervous MP with a marginal seat, a packed weekend diary is essential.

There is the weekly – or twice weekly – advice surgery and then obligatory party fundraisers; being seen in the local supermarket, churches and mosques, at summer fetes, football matches, funerals, factory gates, concerts, schools, old folks' homes and hospitals; campaigning with local councillors; supporting local protests; laying wreaths on Remembrance Day; turning on the Christmas lights; being around for visiting royalty or political celebrities.

The constituency advice surgery is often dismissed as 'social work' but can be crucial and rewarding. There will invariably be someone who desperately needs help, trapped in a web of bureaucracy surrounding welfare benefits, immigration and asylum or special needs provision, or is stranded overseas or in prison. There is a widespread belief in the magical potential of a letter on MP's headed notepaper and that MPs have the ear of people in power. Then, there are the 'regulars' whose problems have gone on for years, even decades, or who lurch from one crisis to another and come to the MP for therapy rather than help.

There are others who should be seeing a local councillor (over a planning application, a dropped curb, a disabled parking bay, overcrowded housing, a place at a popular local school or an overgrown tree) but who believe that the MP is more likely to get a result. Then there are also venomous neighbour disputes, unresolved complaints and litigants with hopeless cases. The MP is expected to listen patiently without committing to solving the insoluble.

Many constituents haven't heard of the Citizens Advice or assume that the MP is a deluxe version of the same. My advice has been sought over the years on: medical issues – from breast enlargement to mental illness (I am the other kind of doctor); tangled personal finances, criminal, family and corporate legal problems (I am not a lawyer); and choice of career, school and college. An eagerness to help can lead to friction with councillors and local professionals; an unwillingness to help feeds a reputation for aloofness. Boris Johnson is credited with revealing **'the dreadful truth is that when people come to see their MP, they have run out of better ideas'**. But don't despise this work; when you look back on your years in Parliament, your biggest achievement may well have been to help turn a few people's lives around.

You will also have a mailbag – now an email box (unless you are a dinosaur or desperate to escape your constituents): local people giving their views. My record haul was of thousands of letters, cards and emails urging me to stop foxhunting. The only foxes in Twickenham are the urban kind that raid rubbish bins. So hunting could hardly be described as a local issue. But the concerned constituents would expect a reply supporting a ban, preferably personalised. And if you are sending out a standard letter drafted by someone else, it pays to read it; I suffered considerable political damage from my standard reply on badger culling, in which I unwisely

cited the minister's view that, in surviving the cull, the
badgers had 'unfairly moved the goalposts'.

THE DAY JOB IN WESTMINSTER

*'I slept for five hours this afternoon in the library
of the House of Commons. A deep House of
Commons sleep. There is no sleep to compare with
it: rich, deep and guilty'*
Henry Channon

Some old-timers long for the days of all-night sittings
and an afternoon siesta in the library, but the arrival of
more women and demands for family-friendly working
have led to more sensible and predictable hours. But this
is not a nine-to-five job. There are, furthermore, many
more things to do than there is time available.

You should spend some time in the chamber,
though, after a while, you start to wonder why. To participate, requires some understanding of procedure.
The rule book of *Erskine May*, compiled by the
nineteenth-century Commons clerk Thomas Erskine
May, is the bible of procedure and those MPs who
have taken the trouble to absorb it can act as a powerful brake on arrogant ministers trying to push through
ill-considered legislation. Like most organisations,
however, Parliament also has its procedural bores and
barrack-room lawyers. But they have their uses, as in
the endless manoeuvring over Brexit legislation.

Those, like me, who were too impatient to bother with procedure, were less effective as a result.

Ritual matters too. The requirement to refer to other members indirectly (the Honourable Member for X); to avoid 'unparliamentary language', like 'liar'; to interrupt only when allowed by the Speaker; to sit down when the Speaker is on his/her feet – these rules can seem petty. But in a Parliament which is very tribal and sometimes beset by bad temper and anger, genuine or synthetic, the rules ensure a modicum of civilised behaviour. There are still some very partisan politicians who fit the description of Henry Adams: **'Politics as a practice, whatever its professions, has always been the systematic organisation of hatreds.'** And beneath the elaborate courtesy some are following Robert Kennedy's advice: **'Always forgive your enemies – but never forget their names.'**

The new member quickly learns, however, that the weekly bunfight of Prime Minister's Questions, the special parliamentary occasions like the Budget and big set-piece debates are untypical. The chamber is usually thinly populated; speeches are invariably devoid of interest, originality or wit, and the 'audience' of fellow MPs is half asleep or fiddling with an iPhone. Even for an important debate on a highly topical subject, the House will be largely empty after the front benches have spoken. Backbenchers will be allowed a few, strictly timed, minutes speaking to a handful of other MPs.

That is the context in which the new MP makes a maiden speech, which by tradition is not interrupted. (A notable exception to this was Disraeli, who, in response to being shouted down durin... dered presciently, **'The time wi... hear me.'**) The convention is that a... with a guided tour of the constituency... former MP however insincere. Mine was pendence of the Bank of England and I w... a nicely bound copy celebrating the event. The Hou.. was empty, however, save for a queue of other MPs waiting to deliver their own maiden speeches. I was cheered by the praise I got from the next speaker, but was told that such praise is given to every maiden speech, however dire.

For some MPs, the maiden speech is like uncorking a bottle, to be followed by endless speeches, interruptions of others' speeches, questions and points of order. Robert Maxwell, when he was MP for Buckingham, became infamous for his total lack of self-awareness. He and others failed to heed the maxim, attributed to Disraeli: **'It is much better that the House should wonder why you do not speak than why you do.'**

It is the tribe and the regular meeting with party colleagues which provides a sense of direction and political context. Clearly, a meeting of 300 Conservatives will have a different feel from a meeting of 50 Nationalists or a dozen Lib Dems. But it is at these meetings that political differences are aired, voting intentions agreed and MPs get a sense of the bigger political picture.

It is also through the party caucus and the party whips that a new MP will quickly discover the limits of their independence. The party hierarchy expects you to

.y .oyal and not make waves. Apart from promotion, inducements include 'fact-finding' foreign trips, constituency visits from the party leader and the award of gongs and peerages at the end of a career. Principled or career rebels may be resistant to obvious bribery but, nonetheless, are keen to avoid being given the worst offices on the estate or being allocated the most tedious committees. It is also in the party caucus that MPs understand that, **'The difference between a caucus and a cactus is that, with a cactus, the pricks are on the outside.'**

You will need to decide, early on, between being a 'loyalist' or a rebel. The usual assumption is that being a loyalist is the way to pursue a career; as Lloyd George put it: **'If you want to succeed in politics, you must keep your conscience firmly under control.'** But loyalty can be taken to excess, as Neil Kinnock observed: **'Loyalty is a fine quality but in excess it fills political graveyards.'** Jeremy Corbyn was a noted and unapologetic party rebel on many issues but came to lead the Labour Party.

CAREER PATHS

Armed with a rudimentary knowledge of procedure, parliamentary manners and what party managers expect of you, you can get to work. The first potential pitfall to be navigated is the risk of running round like a demented fly, and you must choose how best to allocate your time.

Local Champion. For many newcomers, the focus must be on constituency matters. You may have to prioritise local issues, having a narrow majority to defend. The constituency may also be a natural comfort zone for someone who grew up locally and came into politics via the local council. There may be a big local issue – a threatened hospital closure; a big employer in peril; a serious flooding problem; a bypass battle – and you will be expected to take a lead, questioning ministers and, if lucky enough to win the chance in a ballot, to raise the issue in Prime Minister's Questions. Your comments must be relayed to the local paper, radio and TV station, lest the locals have failed to notice their hyperactive MP.

Campaigner. Some MPs come with a cause or adopt one out of idealistic commitment, or because it is a big issue locally, or a lobbying company has made it worthwhile. Parliament is a good vehicle for a campaign. When Tam Dalyell was in the House he would invariably ask about the sinking of the *Belgrano*. David

Tredinnick managed to turn the most improbable sub-ject into an intervention on homeopathic medicines. Andrew Mitchell became recognised for interventions around the aid programme; Bill Cash for indefatigable campaigning on Europe; Stella Creasy for feminist causes; Caroline Lucas on green issues.

Occasionally, an MP makes history, such as when the Labour MP Leo Abse got through a bill to decrimi-nalise homosexuality and the Liberal MP David Steel legislated to liberalise abortion. My own bid for such immortality, with a bill on assisted dying, my having drawn number three in the ballot of MPs, sadly failed when a general election was called, preventing its being debated.

Scrutiny. An important job is 'holding the govern-ment to account'. You bombard the government with written or oral questions or freedom of information requests all designed to outwit a government whose default position is to conceal information or to lie. To my mind, the most useful, and fun, work is on a select committee, where you can cross-question ministers and officials, and independent voices, at length. To be nomi-nated, however, you need support from the party whips (again).

Legislator. Textbooks tell innocent students that an MP's main role in life is to improve legislation. But I confess, I have met very few MPs whose eyes light up at the thought of sitting on a bill committee scrutinising legislation or – outside of impassioned debates, as on Brexit – see themselves, primarily, as legislators. Governments with a majority in the Commons effectively control the legislative agenda; though, very occasionally, a determined and enterprising MP can throw a spanner in the works, as when George Cunningham, a London-based Scot, stalled Scottish devolution for a generation.

Although MPs may have little interest in the detail of legislation passing through Parliament, much of parliamentary business involves voting on it. The regular ringing of bells signals a vote and MPs troop along to the chamber to do so, which is good for keeping fit but wastes a substantial part of the parliamentary day. MPs vote overwhelmingly as advised by the party whips and only the very conscientious will have any idea what they are voting on. Some MPs build a career by following the advice of Asquith: **'The first, if not the whole, duty of the private member of the House of Commons is to speak as little and vote as often as he can.'**

A Job in Government. Many MPs enter Parliament with the main, and sometimes single-minded, ambition of entering government as a minister. I will deal later with the subject of the 'greasy pole'. But there are ways of signalling to government whips or the party leadership, early on, that there is a rising star on the way up.

Political hopefuls can make their presence felt in essentially one of two ways. One is by making a well-timed and brilliant intervention – a question, intervention or speech which catches the attention of ministers, whips, lobby journalists and sketch writers. But this requires luck as well as talent. The other, more common route is obsequiousness: congratulating ministers on their achievements; lambasting and ridiculing the opposition; asking questions considered 'helpful' by the party whips; being ultra-loyal when there are difficult divisions; doing time on tedious committees; issuing press statements parroting 'the line'. The opposition benches cry 'give him a job' and the crawlers usually get something.

I was elected by a bunch of fat, stupid, ugly old ladies that watch soap operas, play bingo, read tabloids and don't know the metric system.
Tom Alciere, when elected to the New Hampshire state legislature

I am simply a bullet fired by the Colne Valley workers against the establishment.
Victor Grayson

Sir, the atrocious crime of being a young man, which the honourable gentleman has, with such spirit and decency, charged me, I shall neither attempt to palliate nor deny; but content myself with wishing that I may be one of those whose follies may cease with their youth, and not of those who continue ignorant in spite of age and experience.

William Pitt the Younger, rebutting Horace Walpole after his election to Parliament

Not merely a chip off the old block, but the block itself.

Edmund Burke, on Pitt the Younger's maiden speech

Say what you have to say, don't quote Latin and sit down.

The Duke of Wellington, when asked his advice on how to speak in the House of Commons

I am a novel principle – here to be endured.

Nancy, Lady Astor (first woman MP to take her seat) in her maiden speech

*I am now here in Congress ... I am at liberty
to vote as my conscience and judgement dictate
to be right, without the yoke of any party on me,
or the driver at my heels, whip in hand,
commanding me to go ge-wo-haw, just at
his pleasure.*
Davy Crockett

*The new Congressman always spends the first
week wondering how he got there, and the rest of
the time wondering how the other members got
there.*
Saturday Evening Post

*The perfection of parliamentary style is to utter
platitudes with a grave and informing air; and if a
little pomposity may be superadded, the House will
recognise the speaker as a statesman.*
George W E Russell

*Newly elected MP, pointing to the benches opposite:
I see that is where the enemy sit.
Elderly colleague: Those are your adversaries.
Your enemies are behind you.*

Parliament will train you to talk; and above all things to hear, with patience, unlimited quantities of foolish talk.

Thomas Carlyle

Today for the first time I really liked it; boredom passed and a glow of pleasure filtered through me. But I wish I understood what I was voting for.

Henry Channon

When you stand up to speak, the bench in front of you seems to catch you just below the knee and gives you the impression that you are about to fall over.

Harold Macmillan

A speaker who doesn't strike oil in ten minutes should stop boring.

Lord Mancroft

Young man, dinna put too much meat in your pie!

James Maxton

If you can't ride two horses at once, you shouldn't be in the circus.

James Maxton

They never open their mouths without subtracting from the sum of human knowledge.

Speaker Thomas Reed on the US House of Representatives

Our great democracies still tend to think that a stupid man is more likely to be honest than a clever man, and our politicians take advantage of this prejudice by pretending to be even more stupid than nature made them.

Bertrand Russell

[The political mind] is a strange mixture of vanity and timidity, of an obsequious attitude at one time and a delusion of grandeur at another time. The political mind is the product of men in public life who have been twice spoiled. They have been spoiled with praise and they have been spoiled with abuse.

Calvin Coolidge

Don't do or say things you would not like to see on the front page of the Washington Post.

Donald Rumsfeld

A politician is a statesman who approaches every question with an open mouth.

Adlai Stevenson

We all know what Parliament is, and we are all ashamed of it.

Robert Louis Stevenson

In Mexico, an air conditioner is called a politician because it makes a lot of noise but doesn't work very well.
Len Deighton

The best time to listen to a politician is when he is on a street corner, in the rain, late at night, when he's exhausted. Then he doesn't lie.
Theodore H White

The right to be heard does not automatically include the right to be taken seriously.
Hubert Humphrey

Since a politician never believes what he says, he is surprised when others believe him.
Charles de Gaulle (attrib.)

Making a speech on economics is like pissing down your leg. It seems hot to you, but it never does to anyone else.
Lyndon B Johnson

I would rather be a little nobody, than to be an evil somebody.
Abraham Lincoln

Don't be an amateur. The job of being a professional politician, in spite of the odium which some persons have falsely attached to it, is a high and difficult one.
Henry Cabot Lodge

If you want a friend in Washington, get a dog.
Adage

A man who puts politics first is not fit to be called a civilised being, let alone a Christian.
Lord Hailsham

Success does not consist in never making mistakes, but in never making the same one a second time.
George Bernard Shaw

Politicians are the same the world over. They promise to build a bridge even where there is no river.

Nikita Khrushchev

Men may be popular without being ambitious, but there is rarely an ambitious man who does not try to be popular.

Lord North

Political language – and with variations this is true of all political parties from Conservatives to Anarchists – is designed to make lies sound truthful and murder respectable.

George Orwell

There seem to me very few facts, at least ascertainable facts, in politics.

Robert Peel

One of the things politics has taught me is that men are not a reasoned or reasonable sex.

Margaret Thatcher

I wish politicians would go out and get another sensible job and spend less time telling us all what to do and how to live.

Jeremy Irons

The art of politics consists in knowing precisely when it is necessary to hit an opponent slightly below the belt.

Konrad Adenauer

A gentleman will blithely do in politics what he would kick a man downstairs for doing in ordinary life.

Lord Rosebery

Never explain. Your friends do not need it and your enemies will not believe you anyway.

Elbert Hubbard

When a man assumes a public trust, he should consider himself as public property.

Thomas Jefferson (attrib.)

5

THE GREASY POLE

'I have climbed to the top of the greasy pole'
Benjamin Disraeli, on becoming prime minister

*'If you take yourself seriously in politics,
you've had it'*
Lord Carrington

If you are making a good impression, you will get a summons to see the chief whip – or, even better, the party leader – to be told that your talent and potential has been spotted and you are to be offered a job. You have reached base camp on the climb up the greasy pole.

THE FIRST STEP

'The ministers of kings should learn to moderate their ambition. The higher they elevate themselves

*above their proper sphere, the greater the danger
that they will fall*
Louis XIV

The first step on the ladder of government is to be a PPS (parliamentary private secretary) to a minister: an unpaid role acting as 'eyes and ears' and generally helping the minister function effectively in Parliament. To confuse matters, there is also a PPS who is the senior civil servant (principal private secretary) managing the minister's private office in the department, a PS (permanent secretary), the top civil servant in the department, and a PUS (parliamentary undersecretary) who is a junior member of the ministerial team under the secretary of state (the boss), and then ministers of state.

To be a PPS to a powerful and rising Cabinet minister is often a stepping stone to bigger things. But not all PPSs are equal. There are currently 43 PPSs. Whilst being attached to a Cabinet star may be a passport to greatness, to be linked to an obscure minister of state on a downward career trajectory is as low as it can get in the career hierarchy. A PPS has no salary and only one weapon: a resignation on principle at a very awkward time.

The next step beyond PPS status is a junior rung on the ministerial ladder. Normally making it a big event, part of a climactic ministerial reshuffle. In the desperate days of Theresa May's premiership, however, with ministers resigning regularly over Brexit issues, PPSs were having to be pressed into ministerial service. A junior ministerial role will, moreover, vary greatly in importance. To be economic secretary to the Treasury – number five in the Treasury team – has a status and career potential far ahead of, say, the number three in the Department for Work and Pensions or Department for Digital, Culture, Media and Sport (though the latter may involve free tickets for big nights at Wembley or the Royal Opera House).

One job which appears very lowly is that of a junior member of the whips team, with none of the glamour of ministerial visits or a big office or having lots of civil servants running around after you. But junior whips have power over their colleagues, knowledge of their strengths and weaknesses and unparalleled opportunities for networking. Not for nothing did John Major and Edward Heath before him build a prime ministerial career in the whips' office.

THE NEXT STEP

'Successful democratic politicians are insecure and intimidated men. They advance politically only as they can placate, appease, bribe, seduce, bamboozle or otherwise manage to manipulate the demanding and threatening elements in their constituencies'
Walter Lippmann

Beyond the foothills of ministerial life, as a PPS, is a serious ministerial appointment as a PUS or a minister of state. You will then have a specific job within the departmental team of ministers: a private office of civil servants and a responsibility for appearing at the despatch box and taking a share of questions, introducing or concluding debates in the designated area of responsibility and steering through pieces of legislation.

There is more pay, access to a ministerial car (possibly), official visits at home and abroad and the opportunity to shine and impress those higher up the greasy pole. There are also chores, like responding to debates when there may be only a couple of MPs in the chamber or taking through very technical secondary legislation (statutory instruments). Some ministers live in dread of being asked to sum up for the government in debates at the end of the day, reading a speech when noise levels are very high and well-lubricated MPs are wanting some entertainment at the minister's expense (though a debating triumph in that environment can be a passport to promotion).

The real shock, however, will come from first exposure to the department. Once you, as a minister, have found where the loos are and been equipped with passes and keys and met and learnt the names of the private office and other key officials, you will need to take stock of what the new responsibilities are. There is a lot to take in, involving issues of considerable complexity – for example, the rules around benefits; school and university finance; local government funding formulae; asylum and immigration claims. A new health minister said that coming to terms with the acronyms of the NHS was like learning the first 100 characters of Mandarin. Yet, within days, there will be meetings with civil servants and 'stakeholders' who have been immersed in the subject for years and questions in Parliament or from the media on the new subject, replies to which have to be passably coherent.

You may be able to shine by launching some new and popular initiative; ideally something close to the heart of the prime minister. But it is a rare stroke of luck to be allowed to oversee a vaccine roll-out, a new grant scheme for depressed areas or a furlough scheme to save people's jobs. A greater political skill is to spot a popular trend and then **'when the inevitable occurs, claim the credit for it'**. You may, however, be lumbered with responsibility for one of the department's unresolved horror stories: Windrush in the Home Office; cladding at Housing; the fallout from the Post Office Horizon project; delayed and over-budget transport projects or defence contracts; top-secret papers and memory sticks which have gone walkabout. There is blame to be allocated (which may involve colleagues); apologies to be made; angry relatives to be appeased; a hyper-critical select committee to face.

In other words, there are risks as well as opportunities. Keep your wits about you and be mindful of the needs of those above you – remember what US civil rights campaigner Vernon Jordan described as **'the first commandment of politics: Help those who help you.'** A lot depends on the secretary of state, who may be a paragon, happy to share both the glory of success and take the hit if something goes wrong. Or a megalomaniac, a coward and a bully. The carve-up of responsibilities may lead to the minister shining or stagnating or sinking. A good case is that of the vaccines minister, Nadhim Zahawi, who received the credit for the vaccine roll-out, having given the impression in interviews that he at least knew what was going on. His successor, however, disappeared without trace.

A bad experience is that of Chloe Smith who was, as the most junior Treasury minister, sent out to defend George Osborne's decision to cancel a fuel duty increase in 2012 and was badly mauled in a Paxman interview. A happier example in the Treasury was David Gauke, who was so successful in batting away hostile questions in Parliament and from the media that 'uncorking the Gauke' became a valued tactic

There are ministerial stars and disasters. There are many in between and there is a risk of getting stuck at the middle tier of government: not good enough or sufficiently important to merit promotion to the Cabinet; not bad enough or sufficiently insignificant to sack. Above all, try not to get too distracted by your peers as they fall by the wayside. Heed Carlos Wallace's dictum: *'The more you focus on someone's downfall, the less likely you are to rise.'*

NEAR THE TOP OF THE POLE

'There are only two ways of getting into the Cabinet. One is to crawl up the staircase of preferment on your belly; the other is to kick them in the teeth. But for God's sake don't mix the two methods'
Aneurin Bevan

There remains one big hurdle: joining the Cabinet. **'A man in office, and out of the Cabinet, is a mere slave,'** said Thomas Babington Macaulay back in the nineteenth century. Yet today, the distinctiveness of becoming a Cabinet minister has become somewhat diluted. There is now a sizeable number of ministers of state who have important functions in government or need to be appeased after failing to get a Cabinet position and who are allowed to attend Cabinet. There are also Cabinet members whose role is largely decorative – the secretaries of state for Scotland and Wales have seen their powers and functions delegated to devolved government (Northern Ireland also, when Stormont is functioning) – but it would cause a big stink if they were dropped. The unelected 'leader of the Lords' is another decoration.

The British Cabinet hasn't quite achieved the comical status of the Indian Union Cabinet, which at one point was expanded to 80 members to accommodate all the government's allies. But we are getting there. And it is clear from the first few meetings a Cabinet minister attends that this is not where key decisions are made. The business of government is settled through 'bilaterals' between Cabinet colleagues or with the prime minister directly; or, formally, through Cabinet subcommittees. Some of the old conventions, like not commenting publicly on Cabinet discussions, have quietly died; I would always expect to read the following day in the press of any significant Cabinet business.

So, what does the view look like from the top of the greasy pole as opposed to halfway up? There is a bigger range of responsibilities, for one. I was shocked on my introduction to my department to discover that there were six civil servants in my private office preparing material for my evening 'red box' or setting up meetings for me to attend. All of this gives the secretary of state more power over decisions but more difficult, complex issues to understand, more civil servants and 'stakeholders' to get to know and more scope for making mistakes. There is more opportunity for glory and making popular announcements (unless Number 10 decides to upstage you), but, also, more damaging publicity when things go wrong. The buck stops at the top, as I discovered when difficult decisions, as around student tuition fees, had to be delivered to Parliament and the press.

For the few who survive the ministerial obstacle course, and still have the appetite and the energy and the appeal within the party, there is one more step: to be prime minister. Until half a century ago, the process of choosing a prime minister, especially on the Conservative side, was something of a mystery. Alec Douglas-Home appears to have been as mystified as the public as to why he was chosen to run against Harold Wilson in the 1964 election and was somewhat reluctant to do so: **'The doctor, unfortunately, said I was fit.'** The process now is more transparent and competitive. But the odds on a new MP reaching that pinnacle must be of the order of 1,000 to 1. And, for most recent British prime ministers, the experience has not ended well.

Politics is a blood sport.

Aneurin Bevan

I'll always be fond of dear Ted [Heath], but there's no sympathy in politics.

Margaret Thatcher

I can foresee no circumstances in which I would allow my name to go forward for the leadership of the Conservative party.

Michael Heseltine, 1989

John Major . . . being calm and sensible, is infinitely preferable to that dreadful charlatan Heseltine. But John is virtually unknown, too vulnerable to the subtle charge of 'not yet ready for it'.

Alan Clark's diary, 17 November 1990

He who wields the dagger never wears the crown.

Michael Heseltine, after mounting his challenge

The first requirement of a statesman is that he be dull. This is not always easy to achieve.

Lester B Pearson

My chances of being PM are about as good as the chances of finding Elvis on Mars, or my being reincarnated as an olive.

Boris Johnson

Being in politics is like being a football coach. You have to be smart enough to understand the game, and dumb enough to think it is important.

Eugene McCarthy

May my words be soft and low for I may have to eat them.

Norman Lamont's 'political prayer'

If you're in politics and you can't tell when you walk into a room who's for you and who's against you, you're in the wrong line of work.

Lyndon B Johnson

A political career brings out the basest qualities in human nature.

Lord Bryce

I used to say that politics is the second oldest profession, and I have come to know that it bears a gross similarity to the first.

Ronald Reagan

Politics is who gets what, when and how.

Harold Lasswell

It rarely pays in politics to be wise before the event.
Chris Patten

Conservative policy is like Brighton pier – all right as far as it goes, but not much use getting to France.
Neil Kinnock

He went 15 rounds with the English language, and left it slumped, bleeding, over the ropes.
Matthew Parris, on the speech by John Prescott which swung the 1993 Labour Party conference behind John Smith

A politician should have three hats. One for throwing in the ring, one for talking through and one for pulling rabbits out of, if elected.
Carl Sandburg

Always be sincere – whether you mean it
or not.

Charles H Percy

A politician needs the ability to foretell what is
going to happen tomorrow, next week, next month,
and next year. And to have the ability afterwards
to explain why it didn't happen.

Winston Churchill

The Trade Union movement has become,
like the hereditary peerage, an avenue to
political power through which stupid untrained
persons may pass up to the highest office if
only they have secured the suffrages of the
members of a large union. One wonders when
able rascals will discover this open door to
remunerative power.

Beatrice Webb

He is a magnet to all young men,
and I warn you that if you talk to him no
good will come of it.

Clement Attlee on Lord Beaverbrook, to his newly
appointed junior ministers

Thank you, Roy, for your honesty and candour in coming to see me and telling me this. I appreciate it greatly. Now piss off.

Anthony Crosland to Roy Hattersley, on being informed that Hattersley would vote for James Callaghan as Labour leader and not for him

A lie can be halfway round the world before the truth has got its boots on.

C H Spurgeon (taken up by James Callaghan)

If a woman like Eva Perón with no ideals can get that far, think how far I can go with all the ideals that I have.

Margaret Thatcher

The end may justify the means, as long as something justifies the end.

Leon Trotsky

A consensus politician is someone who does something he doesn't believe is right because it keeps people quiet.

John Major

I would rather be right than be president.

Henry Clay

The socialist Norman Thomas agreed, but added:
But at any time, I'm ready to be both.

In your heart you know he's right.
Goldwater's campaign slogan, converted by his opponents to:

In your guts you know he's nuts.

I will make a bargain with the Republicans. If they will stop telling lies about the Democrats, we will stop telling the truth about them.

Adlai Stevenson

I am very proud to be called a pig. It stands for pride, integrity and guts.

Ronald Reagan, encountering left-wing demonstrators as governor of California

Depression is when you are out of work. A recession is when your neighbour loses his job. And a recovery is when Jimmy Carter loses his job.

Ronald Reagan

They've got a point. I don't have any experience of running up a $4 trillion deficit.

Ross Perot to George H W Bush, during the 1992 presidential debates

Don't get mad. Don't get even. Just get elected. THEN get even.

Bill Clinton's political strategist James Carville. Based on Everett Dirksen's Three Laws of Politics:

1. Get elected.

2. Get re-elected.

3. Don't get mad, get even.

I got a mamma who joined the Peace Corps and went to India when she was 68. I got one sister who's a Holy Roller preacher. I got another sister who wears a helmet and rides a motorbike. And I got a brother who thinks he's going to be president. So that makes me the only sane person in the family.

Billy Carter

Asked if he would accept a draft for the 1980 Democratic presidential nomination – not that one was on offer – Representative Morris Udall said:
Only on three conditions. 1. If a star rose in the East. 2. If three men on camels rode up demanding that I run. 3. If their names were Carter, Mondale and Kennedy.

Tomorrow every duchess in London will be wanting to kiss me.
Ramsay MacDonald, on forming the National Government

The opportunity to serve our country. That is all we ask.

The words on John Smith's tombstone, taken from his last ever speech

My husband and I have no intention of hiding our wealth, not like that four-million-dollar – I can't say it but it rhymes with 'rich'.

Barbara Bush, wife of the then vice president, on his Democrat opponent Geraldine Ferraro

I just received the following wire from my generous Daddy – 'Dear Jack, Don't buy a single vote more than necessary. I'm damned if I'm going to pay for a landslide.'

John F Kennedy, 1958

Running for president is like sticking your face in the blade of a fan.

Mike Huckabee

Win or lose, we go shopping after the election.

Imelda Marcos

You won the elections – but I won the count.

Nicaragua's dictator Anastasio Somoza

When I am the candidate, I run the campaign.

Richard Nixon

*I will totally accept the results [of the 2016 election]
if I win.*
Donald Trump

He reminds every woman of her first husband.
Adage originally applied to Thomas E Dewey

---

*If you have not chosen me by secret ballot,
neither have I gained office by any secret promises.
I have not campaigned either for the presidency
or the vice presidency. I have not subscribed
to any partisan platform. I am indebted to no
man, and only to one woman – my dear wife –
as I begin this very difficult job.*
Gerald Ford, taking the oath of office after the resignation
of President Nixon

Winston is back.
Signal to all ships of the Royal Navy from the Admiralty
on Churchill's return as first lord, 1939

---

*It is some measure of the tightness of the
magic circle on this occasion that neither the
Chancellor of the Exchequer nor the leader of the
House of Commons had any inkling of what was
happening.*
Iain Macleod, on the 'emergence' of Lord Home as prime
minister

My movements to the chair of government will be accompanied by feelings not unlike those of a culprit who is going to the place of execution.

George Washington

Boys, if ever you pray, pray for me now. I don't know whether you fellows ever had a load of hay fall on you, but when they told me what had happened I felt like the moon, the stars and the planets had fallen on me.

Harry S Truman to reporters, on being told FDR had died and he was president

6

GOVERNMENT AND POWER

*'We know that no one ever seizes power with the
intention of relinquishing it'*
George Orwell

You have made it to government. Power! Or so you
thought.

When you are asked to join the Cabinet, you may
have some fanciful idea about 'Cabinet government'.
Maybe you read about it in a textbook. But in recent
decades the term 'prime ministerial government' is more
accurate, but where the prime minister is constrained by
powerful ministers (the chancellor in particular) and the
parliamentary party. In addition, there are three powerful
devolved governments. With big parliamentary majorities, governments have real power, but with minority
government – as under Theresa May or in the 1974–79

Labour government – a lot of power rests with MPs outside government and with minority parties. Then there is formal coalition with which I was familiar: powerful and effective government but subject to a lot of horse-trading between two parties. Different election outcomes will determine who calls the shots, but with some common elements.

PROMISES, PROMISES, PROMISES

'Don't say in power what you say in opposition.
If you do, you only have to carry out what
the other fellows have found impossible'
John Galsworthy

You don't arrive in power with a clean sheet of paper on which to write your programme and implement policy. All kinds of promises will have been made during an election campaign or before which it would be embarrassing or worse to break. The phrase 'it's in your manifesto' can be hung around the neck of any new government wanting to resile from commitments made in the heat of an electoral battle – not just by opponents but by party supporters who can argue that their support was conditional on promises being honoured.

One of the more notorious promises was George H W Bush's televised pledge: **'Read My Lips: No New Taxes.'** Bush was leading a party which believed above all in small government and low taxes, following in the tradition of

Ronald Reagan who said: *'The most fearsome words in the English language are: "I'm from the government and I'm here to help".'* After Bush won and gained office, the budget deficit (inherited from Reagan) deteriorated and the Democrat-controlled Congress proposed higher taxes. Bush compromised but was unable to avoid signing up to tax increases. Bill Clinton, his opponent when he sought re-election, mercilessly mocked the broken promise and defeated Bush after one term.

Senator Eugene McCarthy once warned, *'It is dangerous for a national candidate to say things people might remember.'* There is no shortage of examples on this side of the Atlantic of politicians forgetting that other people might remember what they had said. Boris Johnson made an explicit commitment not to raise income tax or VAT, which proved very awkward when the fiscal situation deteriorated due to the Covid pandemic. The subsequent rise in National Insurance has been seen as bad faith as well as bad policy. David Cameron probably thought he was on safe ground promising a referendum on the EU to head off rising support for UKIP on the right of the Conservative Party. He disastrously miscalculated the risk of having to deliver a referendum and then losing it.

A similar disaster befell the Liberal Democrats in that government. A system of internal 'democracy' led to party activists, rather than the leadership, framing manifesto commitments. One such commitment was to phase out tuition fees introduced by the previous

Labour government. The leadership then made a widely publicised pledge not to raise tuition fees. In government, the pledge was not compatible with the government's overriding objective of cutting the budget deficit substantially and had to be abandoned, with a big increase in fees. The loss of trust which followed the breaking of the pledge contributed to my party's subsequent electoral heavy defeat. I felt the pain of being involved in the pledge, the policy U-turn and the defeat.

The problem created by manifesto commitments tailored to party campaigning and conviction rather than the constraints of government has historically been a major problem for the Labour Party, whose activists have long insisted on promises of nationalisation. But in 1997, the Blair government came up with a novel and successful solution to the problems of matching pledges and power. A short, five-point pledge card was presented as the party's offer, carefully worded to involve modest commitments. In office, the programme was deliverable.

MONEY, MONEY, MONEY

'Whichever party is in office, the Treasury is always in power'
Harold Wilson

Most governments, at some stage, run into financial difficulties trying to reconcile popular policies of more public spending or cutting taxes with the need to keep any budget deficit, and public debt, within sustainable limits. One of the first things you learn in office is that the most powerful job in government, after the prime minister (and sometimes before), is the Chancellor of the Exchequer and that the Treasury is the most powerful government department.

Post-war Labour governments have run into a succession of budget crises: the 1951 austerity budget to pay for the Korean War, which precipitated the resignation of Aneurin Bevan and Harold Wilson; the 1976 crisis when Chancellor Denis Healey turned to the IMF for help; and the end of the Brown government when the public finances were badly hit by the banking crisis. After the last of these, outgoing chief secretary to the Treasury Liam Byrne left a note for his successor, saying, **'I'm afraid there is no money.'** He was echoing a former Conservative chancellor, Reginald Maudling, who in 1964 handed over to his Labour government successor, with the phrase: **'Sorry to leave it in such a mess, old cock.'** In neither case did history treat their outbreak of honestly at all kindly.

British post-war history has been one of popular fiscal indulgence followed by periods of unpopular austerity. Margaret Thatcher, by contrast, tried to popularise budget discipline by invoking the prudent housewife: **'How very popular to say, "Spend more on this"; "Spend more on that". And of course, we all have our favourite causes . . . Someone has to add up the figures. Every business has to do it. Every housewife has to do it. And every government has to do it.'** Her own government, however, went through a boom-and-bust cycle like any other, partly originating in aggressive, unaffordable tax cutting.

The Treasury maintains its grip over politicians through a combination of spending control through departmental spending limits, negotiated over a three- or four-year period, and the chancellor's powers of taxation. Michael Heseltine observed that **'the Treasury never sleeps'**. Harold Wilson complained, as above, **'Whatever party is in office, the Treasury is always in power.'** And at least Wilson was a trained economist with a background in government, unlike his predecessor, Sir Alec Douglas-Home, who admitted to using matchsticks to help clarify budgetary arithmetic.

The complexity of economic policy and the need to institutionalise discipline have led to subcontracting out monetary policy to an operationally independent central bank (the Bank of England, the European Central Bank, the US Federal Reserve) and to have independent assessment of budgetary policy (in the UK, the Office for Budget Responsibility). The underlying assumption is that financial and wider economic judgements need to be guided by experts as well as professional civil servants.

CIVIL SERVANTS AND EXPERTS

'All my life I've known better than to depend on the experts. How could I have been so stupid, to let them go ahead?'
John F Kennedy, after the Bay of Pigs fiasco

The implementation of policy occurs through the civil service, augmented by experts such as scientific and health advisers. The relationship between government ministers and civil servants was explored and lampooned in the satirical programme *Yes Minister*, which captured the mutual dependence, the difference of interests, the affection and the suspicion which runs through the relationship.

The civil service is apolitical and its selection and promotion should be on merit. It has evolved from a system characterised as follows by an official report in the mid-nineteenth century: **'Admission to the Civil Service is indeed eagerly sought after but it is for the unambitious, indolent or incapable that it is chiefly desired.'** More recent cynicism has centred on the way clever and cunning civil servants supposedly run the government in their own interests and manipulate inexperienced and rather naïve ministers, who are out of their depth. Ideologues frequently invoke this argument to explain why their big ideas and simple solutions to complex problems have stalled or failed.

By contrast, the minister's job is **'to tell the Civil Servant what the Public will not stand'**, according to nineteenth-century Liberal statesman William Harcourt. And to decide between difficult options and sell the one that he/she has chosen. Having worked with a civil service team for five years in a very big, complex government department, I emerged with enhanced respect for the officials and subscribe to the assessment of a recent Cabinet minister, William Waldegrave, that **'It is the** definition of a feeble minister if he blames the civil service for not delivering his policies.'

This brings us to experts. Harold Macmillan wrote that, 'Fearing the weakness of democracy, men have often sought safety in technocrats. There is nothing new in this. It is as old as Plato. But frankly, the idea is not attractive to the British. We have not overthrown the divine right of kings to fall down before the divine right of experts.' This sense of distrust was captured a generation later by Michael Gove: 'The people of this country have had enough of experts.' He was referring to work on the economic impact of Brexit by the Government Economic Service. But experts from the 'hard sciences' can be controversial at the same time as being right. Britain was led through the pandemic by political decisions informed by public health officials and epidemiologists, which was a better basis for decisions than – say – President Trump's adoption of quack cures and conspiracy theories. Government scientists, collaborating with academic researchers, have ensured that policies on climate change are based on an emerging scientific consensus, rather than vested interests or maverick articles on the internet.

One new phenomenon has been the emergence of SPADs (special advisers). Some traditionalists believe that they undermine the civil service. My experience is the opposite; they prevent civil servants being dragged into party political arguments and internal arguments within parties and are invaluable. I like the summary of one of the SPADs who worked in my department (for the Conservative minister David Willetts), Nick Hillman: **'Special advisers are like poisoners: either famous or good at their job.'** And hiring people who are good at their job is a key aspect of leadership to which I now turn.

The civil service has a difficulty for every solution.

Lord Samuel

You may fool some of the people some of the time; you can even fool some of the people all the time; but you can't fool all of the people all the time.
Variously attributed to Abraham Lincoln and P T Barnum

It is customary in democratic countries to deplore expenditure on armaments as conflicting with the requirements of the social services. There is a tendency to forget that the most important social service that a government can do for its people is to keep them alive and free.
Marshal of the RAF Sir John Slessor

The art of taxation consists in so plucking the goose as to obtain the largest possible amount of feathers with the smallest possible amount of hissing.
Louis XIV's finance minister Jean-Baptiste Colbert (attrib.)

If we can find the money to kill people, we can find the money to help people.

Tony Benn

I have been trying to work out which has cost Britain more. The Second World War, or Tony Benn.

One of Benn's civil servants to Anthony Sampson

While the people retain their virtue and vigilance, no administration, by an extreme of wickedness or folly, can very seriously injure the government in the short space of four years.

Abraham Lincoln (proved wrong by Donald Trump?)

Nor ought one to rely exclusively on the civil service department's famous 'List of the Great and the Good', all of whose members ... are aged fifty-three, live in the south-east, have the right accent and belong to the Reform Club.

Anthony Sampson

Being Chancellor is not a woman's job. There's a difference between the sexes, and people who don't know that don't know what people are like with their clothes off. So there.

Denis Healey

During a general election, civil servants do what they do the rest of the time: get drunk and have affairs.

Ken Clarke

We know there are known knowns: there are things we know we know. We also know there are known unknowns: that is to say we know there are things we know we don't know. But there are also unknown unknowns – the ones we don't know we don't know.

Donald Rumsfeld

Standing up to one's enemies is commendable, but give me the man who can stand up to his friends.

William Gladstone

Politics is the art of looking for trouble, finding it everywhere, diagnosing it wrongly, and applying unsuitable remedies.

Sir Ernest Benn

No more distressing moment can ever face a British government than that which requires it to come to a hard, fast and specific decision.

Barbara Tuchman

It is easier to cancel a nuclear submarine than a civil servant's parking place.

Simon Jenkins

When we got into office, the thing that surprised me most was to find that things were just as bad as we'd been saying they were.

John F Kennedy

The art of the possible.

The title of R A Butler's memoir, and a phrase associated over time with cynicism. The quote originated with Bismarck, who defined politics as **'the doctrine of the possible, the attainable ... the art of the next best.'**

J K Galbraith disagreed:

Politics is not the art of the possible. It consists in choosing between the disastrous and the unpalatable.

___

And to Arthur C Clarke:

Because politics is the science of the possible, it only appeals to second-rate minds. The first raters only interested in the impossible.

___

Two kinds of chairs to go with two kinds of ministers: one sort that folds up instantly, the other sort goes round and round in circles.

The fictional Bernard Woolley in *Yes Minister*

___

What you get in Sibelius, for the greater part of the time, is an extreme reticence and a slow delivery; and that, of course, is very popular in England. It is our tradition. We get it, possibly, from the government.

Sir Thomas Beecham

___

Parliament without a whips' office is like a city without sewage.

Robert Atkins

___

The House of Commons allows itself to be led, but does not like to be driven, and is apt to turn on those who attempt to drive it.

Lord Palmerston

Government exists to protect us from each other. Where government has gone beyond its limits is in deciding to protect us from ourselves.

Ronald Reagan

Necessity is the plea for every infringement of human freedom.

William Pitt the Younger

I am not going to go round the country stirring up apathy.

William Whitelaw

The cocktail glass is one of the most powerful instruments of government.

Kenneth Crawford

If you've got them by the balls, their hearts and minds will follow.

Motto on the wall of the office of Nixon White House aide Charles Colson

---

Reform? Reform? Aren't things bad enough already?

Duke of Wellington (attrib.)

An honest man can feel no pleasure in the exercise of power over his fellow citizens.

Thomas Jefferson

I have difficulty in looking humble for extended periods of time.

Henry Kissinger

Henry [Kissinger]'s idea of sex is to slow the car down to 30 miles an hour when he drops you off at the door.

Barbara Howard

I do not want a honeymoon with you. I want a good marriage.

Gerald Ford to the US Congress, on taking office

When I'm sitting on the Woolsack in the House of Lords I amuse myself by saying 'bollocks', sotto voce, to the bishops.

Lord Hailsham

Rising unemployment and the recession have been the price we have had to pay to get inflation down. It has been a price worth paying.

Norman Lamont, 1991

It does no harm to throw the occasional man overboard, but it does not do much good if you are steering full speed for the rocks.

Sir Ian Gilmour, after being sacked by Mrs Thatcher

The Crown is, according to the saying, the 'fountain of honour', but the Treasury is the spring of business.

Walter Bagehot

The weekly meetings between the Queen and Mrs Thatcher – both the same age – are dreaded by at least one of them. The relationship is the more difficult because the roles seem confused; the Queen's style is more matter-of-fact and domestic, while it is Mrs Thatcher (who is taller) who bears herself like a queen.

Anthony Sampson

The whole life of English politics is the action and reaction between the Ministry and the Parliament.

Walter Bagehot

One thing the House will never forgive, and that is if a Minister misleads it.

Stanley Baldwin

When the Government of the day and the Opposition of the day take the same side, one can be almost sure that some great wrong is at hand.

George W E Russell

When I first came into Parliament, Mr Tierney, a great Whig authority, used always to say that the duty of an Opposition was very simple – it was to oppose everything, and propose nothing.
Lord Derby

This administration is going to do for sex what the last one did for golf.
Kennedy White House insider as JFK took over from Eisenhower

When I read economic documents, I have to have a box of matches and start moving them into position, to illustrate and simplify the points to myself.
Sir Alec Douglas-Home

The codeword of my administration will be 'reality'.

Ed Koch

An open mind is like an open sewer.
Ernest Bevin

The first Permanent Secretary I ever met told me he always judged a Secretary of State on whether he brought home the groceries.
Ken Clarke

If the government is big enough to give you all you want, it is big enough to take it away.
Barry Goldwater

Labour is the party of law and order in Britain today: tough on crime; tough on the causes of crime.
Tony Blair

Sometimes it is better to lose and do the right thing than to win and do the wrong thing.
Tony Blair

Whichever way you decide, before long, you will wish you had done the opposite.
Australian prime minister William Hughes, often to his Cabinet

The only good government is a bad one in a hell of a fright.
Joyce Cary, *The Horse's Mouth*

A *week* is a long time in politics.
Harold Wilson

But compare Joseph Chamberlain:
In politics there is no use in looking beyond the next fortnight.

There are no necessary evils in government. Its evils exist only in its abuses.

Andrew Jackson

Great innovations should not be forced on slender majorities.
Thomas Jefferson

Government has no other end but the protection of property.
John Locke

What is a government for except to dictate? If it does not dictate, then it is not a government.

David Lloyd George

The nearest thing on this earth to immortality is a government bureau.

James F Byrnes

If Moses had been a committee, the Israelites would never have got across the Red Sea.

Salvation Army general William Booth

Were we directed from Washington when to sow and when to reap, we should soon want bread.

Thomas Jefferson

The true art of government lies in not governing too much.

Bishop Jonathan Shipley of St Asaph

We are all imperfect. We cannot expect perfect government.

William Howard Taft

A bureaucrat is a Democrat who holds a job a Republican wants.

Alben Barkley

Good administration can never save bad policy.
Adlai Stevenson

The official world, the corridors of power, the dilemmas of conscience and egotism – he disliked them all.
C P Snow, *Homecomings*

Power tends to corrupt, and absolute power to corrupt absolutely.

Lord Acton

But Frank Herbert wrote:
Absolute power does not corrupt absolutely, absolute power attracts the corruptible.

Labour failed to fix the roof when the sun was shining.
George Osborne

All modes of government are failures. High hopes were once formed of democracy; but democracy means simply the bludgeoning of the people by the people for the people.

Oscar Wilde

A government is the only known vessel that leaks from the top.

James Reston

It is the duty of Her Majesty's Government not to flap or falter.

Harold Macmillan

Men of power have no time to read; yet the men who do not read are unfit for power.

Michael Foot

A Conservative government is an organised hypocrisy.

Benjamin Disraeli

The trouble with being minister of transport is that it's the only job I know when you are expected to apologise to others when they are late for your meetings.

Paul Channon

The Army will hear nothing of politics from me, and in return I expect to hear nothing of politics from the Army.

Herbert Asquith, on the Curragh Mutiny

Asquith once took the War Office to task for producing three sets of figures:

One to mislead the public, one to mislead the Cabinet, and the third to mislead itself.

In the case of nutrition and health, just as in the case of education, the gentleman in Whitehall really does know better what is good for people, than the people know themselves.

Douglas Jay

He has picked a Cabinet of eight millionaires and a plumber.

Richard Strout, 'TRB', *Christian Science Monitor*, on Eisenhower's first administration

---

When the ground shakes under governments, it is no good their trying to sit still.

Klemens von Metternich

Never believe anything in politics until it has been officially denied.

Otto von Bismarck

The quality of legislation passed to deal with a problem is inversely proportional to the volume of media clamour that brought it on.

G Ray Funkhouser

A government which robs Peter to pay Paul can always depend on the support of Paul.

George Bernard Shaw

The essence of government is power; and power, lodged as it must be in human hands, will ever be liable to abuse.

James Madison

Sometimes, if you want to keep a secret, announce it in the House of Commons.

Chris Patten, noticing the Press Gallery was almost empty

7

LEADERSHIP

'The buck stops here'
Harry S Truman

'Nearly all men can stand adversity, but if you want to test a man's character, give him power'
Abraham Lincoln

'The easiest job in the world. Everyone else has an instrument to play – you just stand there and conduct'
James Callaghan

You think you have what it takes to be a leader? You will only know when you do it. I suggest that paying through the nose to go on a 'leadership course' won't help much. Leading a party, let alone a country, involves different skills from leading a company or a cricket team.

Politics has thrown up inspirational figures like FDR, Mahatma Gandhi and Nelson Mandela. They are great role models. But let me focus on the UK. For many people, Churchill embodies political leadership, not just because of his leadership in the Second World War, but on account of his contribution as a Liberal reformer and as part of the leadership team in the First World War. His oratory would not suit modern tastes but was inspirational in its time. He was aware of the adage, first demonstrated by Julius Caesar, that history is written by the winners. Churchill commented: **'History will be kind to me for I intend to write it.'** He did, in four volumes.

His detractors point to his support for imperialism and occasional use of negative racial stereotypes, but the former was the orthodoxy of the time and in respect of the latter, he took a strong stand against racism during debates on the 1904 Aliens Act and left the Tory Party over the issue.

David Lloyd George probably merits the adjective 'great' as well, for his leadership during the First World War and his role as a Liberal reformer before it. But he was dogged by scandal of various kinds and by personal feuds which led to the break-up of the Liberal Party. And his combative style made enemies. As Margot Asquith commented, **'He could not see a belt without hitting below it.'**

Of politicians who led in peacetime, Clement Attlee was an outstanding figure, though his dry and unprepossessing personality often led to his being underestimated, not least by Churchill, who described him as **'a modest man with much to be modest about'**. His combination of radical but practical socialist action combined with fierce patriotism is a formula Labour leaders strive to emulate to this day.

The other plausible post-war figure for placing in the pantheon of outstanding leaders is Margaret Thatcher. She was, and remains, a very divisive figure, greatly disliked by some of her adversaries for her uncompromising and partisan approach. She was an ideologue who was identified with the statement: **'There is no such thing as society. There are individual men and women and there are families.'** She made a virtue of being the first British woman prime minister: **'If you want something said, ask a man; if you want something done, ask a woman.'** Others made the same point less flatteringly, describing her as 'Attila the Hen'. She usually got her way – **'I don't mind how much my ministers talk provided I get my way in the end'** – and she revelled in her international reputation as uncompromising: **'The lady's not for turning,'** she told the Conservative Party conference, firmly resisting opposition to her plans to liberalise the economy.

Most national leaders, at least in a democracy, come to power as a result of success at the ballot box. But there are numerous cases of people who were outstanding leaders of their parties and election winners but whom history has not treated kindly as national leaders. Harold Wilson won four elections against the Conservatives (and lost one). His political instincts and campaigning skills were widely admired. He united the Labour Party – no mean feat. But his governments were beset by economic crises and his central objective of using technology to raise British productivity was never realised. His achievements include letting his liberal-minded ministers introduce socially liberal legislation, keeping out of the Vietnam War and winning a confirmatory referendum on membership of the EEC. His alleged deviousness, however, earned the comment from David Frost: **'At least you knew where you were with Machiavelli.'**

Tony Blair beat the Conservatives three times (no losses) and more convincingly than Wilson. He knew how to lead: **'I can only go one way, I have no reverse gear.'** His prime ministership, essentially a partnership with Gordon Brown, introduced a rules-based system of economic policy making, a national minimum wage, devolution to the nations of the UK and large investment in health and education. The economic gains were later washed away after the financial crisis of 2008, however. And the issue which will forever define his leadership was the Iraq War. Unpopular and unsuccessful wars have been the political death of other election-winning leaders, as with Anthony Eden after the failed Suez action. Harold Wilson spoke of Eden's **'expensive education: Eton and Suez'**.

Sometimes, successful political leadership isn't just about winning elections. Neil Kinnock could reasonably be credited with rebuilding the Labour Party after the near-death experience of the SDP split but he went on to lose two elections before passing on the leadership. In my party, Paddy Ashdown led the Lib Dems from near extinction to being a serious political force. His successor, Charles Kennedy, described him as **'the only party leader to be a trained killer, but to be fair, Mrs Thatcher was self-taught'**. And Nigel Farage led his anti-EU party, which never won any seats in Parliament, to a position of great influence and ultimately victory in the Brexit referendum. His leadership style may have been unorthodox and undisciplined, but his communication and debating skills, and ability to stay the course, are something of an object lesson in political leadership.

The recent turbulence of British politics is a good illustration of the precariousness of politicians' reputations and how leadership skills that were so successful in one context can fail in another. The road from hero to zero is short.

Boris Johnson is credited with leading the successful 'No' campaign and then winning the 2019 election and 'getting Brexit done' (albeit with some messy leftovers). His leadership style is highly unorthodox, relying on bonhomie, approachability, optimism and humour. It seemed an unbeatable formula despite many mistakes. Eventually, a chaotic lifestyle and complete lack of integrity caught up with him in the Partygate scandal. At the time of writing, his popularity had collapsed, justifying the quote: **'the unchallenged master of the self-inflicted wound'**. But he is still in power with everything to play for.

It is the loneliest job in the world. A prime minister cannot share his ultimate responsibilities.

Stanley Baldwin

Above any other position of eminence, that of prime minister is filled by fluke.

Enoch Powell

I prefer to supervise the whole operation of the government myself, rather than entrust the public business to subordinates, and this makes my duties very great.

James Polk

LEADING AND FOLLOWING

There go the people. I must follow them, for I am their leader.

Attributed to Alexandre Ledru-Rollin, one of the leaders of France's revolution of 1848. Wrongly credited to Andrew Bonar Law

Compare:

You cannot be a leader, and ask other people to follow you, unless you know how to follow, too.

Sam Rayburn

To:

If you are guided by opinion polls, you are not practising leadership – you are practising followship.

Margaret Thatcher

And also with:

I have got you together to hear what I have written down. I do not wish your advice about the main matter – for that I have determined for myself.

Abraham Lincoln to his Cabinet before issuing the Emancipation Proclamation

A great nation is not led by a man who simply repeats the talk of the street corners or the opinions of the newspapers. A nation is led by a man who ... hearing those things, understands them better.

Woodrow Wilson

To succeed pre-eminently in English public life it is necessary to conform either to the public image of a bookie or of a clergyman; Churchill being the perfect example of the former, Halifax of the latter.

Malcolm Muggeridge

Leadership is not about being popular, it's about being right. It's not about going through some shopping centre tripping over TV cords, it's about doing what the country needs.

Paul Keating (on Bob Hawke)

How can a president not be an actor?

Ronald Reagan

On the whole, nobody comes to see you when you are prime minister. The nice people don't come because they don't want to be thought courtiers, and the tiresome people – you don't want to see them.

Harold Macmillan

The main essentials of a successful prime minister are sleep and a sense of history.
Harold Wilson

If you can't convince them, confuse them.

Harry S Truman

In politics it is necessary either to betray one's country or the electorate. I prefer to betray the electorate.
Charles de Gaulle

I have against me the bourgeois, the military and the diplomats, and for me, only the people who take the Métro.
Charles de Gaulle

Let me say for the benefit of those that have allowed themselves to be carried away by the gossip of the past few days: I know what's going on. I am going on.
Harold Wilson

Once when a British prime minister sneezed, men half a world away would blow their noses. Now when a British prime minister sneezes, nobody even says 'Bless you'.
Bernard Levin

I can honestly say that I was never affected by the question of the success of an undertaking. If I felt it was the right thing to do, I was for it regardless of the possible outcome.
Golda Meir

In my experience of the [Australian] Labor Party, the fact that someone is a bastard has never been a disqualification from leadership.
John Button

It was a day when I was preparing a speech to be delivered in praise of the Emperor; there would be a lot of lies in the speech and they would be applauded by those who knew that they were lies.
The Confessions of St Augustine

I would rather consult my valet than the Conservative conference.
Arthur Balfour

It doesn't matter what majority you come in with. You've got just one year when they treat you right.

Lyndon B Johnson

All presidents start out pretending to run a crusade, but after a couple of years they find they are running something much less heroic, more intractable: namely, the presidency.

Alistair Cooke

He aroused every feeling except trust.

A J P Taylor on David Lloyd George

Compare:

Some are born great, some achieve greatness, and some have greatness thrust upon them.

Malvolio in Shakespeare's *Twelfth Night*

And:

If I am a great man, then a good many great men must have been frauds.

Andrew Bonar Law

All the president is is a glorified public relations man who spends his time flattering, kissing and kicking people to get them to do what they are supposed to do anyway.

Harry S Truman

To promote a woman to bear rule, superiority, dominion, or empire, above any Realm, Nation, or City, is repugnant to Nature; contumely to God, a thing most contrarious to his revealed will and approved ordinance; and finally it is the subversion of good order, of all equity and justice.

John Knox

A willingness to consult your senior colleagues indicates a willingness not to proceed with the decision.

Malcolm Fraser

To make a people great it is necessary to send them into battle, even if you have to kick them in the pants.

Benito Mussolini

I count my blessings for the fact that I don't have to go into that pit that John Major stands in, nose-to-nose with the Opposition, all yelling at each other.

George H W Bush, on PMQs

Words can do more than convey policy. They can also convey and create a mood, an attitude, an atmosphere – or an awakening.

John F Kennedy

When power leads a man towards arrogance, poetry reminds him of his limitations.

John F Kennedy

Anything more dull and commonplace it wouldn't be easy to reproduce.

The Times, on Lincoln's Gettysburg Address

I would rather be an opportunist and float than go to the bottom with my principles round my neck.

Stanley Baldwin

He spent his life, with legendary success, in the pursuit of personal glory; and until very recent times this was regarded as a wholly laudable aim.

Peter Green, *Alexander of Macedon* [Alexander the Great]

Murder, robbery, rape, adultery and incest will be openly taught and practised. The air will be rent with the cries of distress, the soil soaked with blood and the nation black with crimes. Where is the heart that can contemplate such a scene without shivering with horror?

The *New-England Courant*, on the election of Thomas Jefferson as president, 1800

If a traveller were informed that such a man was the Leader of the House of Commons, he might begin to comprehend how the Egyptians worshipped an insect.

Benjamin Disraeli on Lord John Russell

Honest in the most odious sense of the word.

Benjamin Disraeli on William Gladstone

My dear McClellan: If you don't want to use the Army I should like to borrow it for a while. Yours respectfully, A. Lincoln.

Abraham Lincoln, when the Civil War had gone uncomfortably quiet

I don't object to the Old Man always having the Ace of Trumps up his sleeve, but merely to his belief that God Almighty put it there.

Henry Labouchère on William Gladstone

Mr Gladstone speaks to me as if I were a public meeting.

Queen Victoria

If Gladstone fell into the Thames, that would be a misfortune, and if anybody pulled him out that, I suppose, would be a calamity.

Benjamin Disraeli

Mr Gladstone read Homer for fun, which I think served him right.

Winston Churchill

Right on most of the big things, wrong on most of the little ones.

Sam Rayburn on Harry S Truman

He was always forgetting he was prime minister. He would ask why people crowded round when he went shopping alone.

Arthur Ponsonby on Henry Campbell-Bannerman

He had about as much backbone as a chocolate éclair.

Theodore Roosevelt on William McKinley

My colleagues tell military secrets to their wives, except Asquith, who tells them to other people's wives.

Lord Kitchener

He is incapable of achieving anything without reducing all around him to be nervous wrecks.

Frances Stevenson, his secretary, mistress and future second wife, on David Lloyd George

---

Fifty per cent genius. Fifty per cent bloody fool.

Clement Attlee on Winston Churchill

He does not care in which direction the car is travelling, so long as he remains in the driving seat.

Lord Beaverbrook on David Lloyd George

He spent his whole life in plastering together the true and the false, and therefrom manufacturing the plausible.

Stanley Baldwin on David Lloyd George

When he launched his scheme for peopling Palestine with Jewish immigrants, I am credibly informed that he did not know there were any Arabs in the country.

Dean Inge on A J Balfour

I remember, when I was a child, being taken to the celebrated Barnum's Circus, which contained an exhibition of freaks and monstrosities; but the exhibit on the programme which I most desired to see was the one described 'The Boneless Wonder'. My parents judged the spectacle would be too revolting and demoralising for my youthful eyes, and I have waited fifty years to see The Boneless Wonder sitting on the Treasury Bench.

Winston Churchill on Ramsay MacDonald

You were given the choice between war and dishonour. You chose dishonour, and you will have war.

Winston Churchill to Neville Chamberlain after the Munich Conference

When the call came for me to form a government, one of my first thoughts was that it should be a government of which Harrow should not be ashamed.

Stanley Baldwin

Decided only to be undecided, resolved to be irresolute, adamant for drift, solid for fluidity, all-powerful to be impotent.

Winston Churchill on Stanley Baldwin

I have nothing to offer but blood, toil, tears and sweat.

Winston Churchill, on taking office

No better than a Mayor of Birmingham, and in a lean year at that.

Lord Hugh Cecil on Neville Chamberlain

Listening to [Neville] Chamberlain is like a visit to Woolworth's; everything in its place, and nothing above sixpence.

Aneurin Bevan

He would kill his own mother just so that he could use her skin to make a drum to beat his own praises.

Margot Asquith on Winston Churchill

I have never accepted what many people have kindly said, namely that I inspired the nation. It was the nation and the race dwelling all round the globe that had the lion's heart. I had the luck to be called upon to supply the roar.

Winston Churchill on his wartime leadership

A sheep in sheep's clothing.
Winston Churchill on Ramsay MacDonald

Feed grubs royal jelly and they become queens.
Winston Churchill on Clement Attlee as prime minister

He seems determined to make a trumpet sound like a tin whistle. He brings to the fierce struggle of politics the tepid enthusiasm of a lazy summer afternoon at a cricket match.
Aneurin Bevan on Clement Attlee

Few thought him even a starter.
There were many who thought themselves smarter.
But he ended PM, CH and OM,
And an earl and a Knight of the Garter.
Clement Attlee, on himself

I never give them hell. I just give them the truth, and they think it's hell.

Harry S Truman

When he did say boo, he said it to the wrong goose and far too roughly.

Harold Wilson on Anthony Eden

The nation's number one Boy Scout.

George Kennan on Dwight D Eisenhower

The only living unknown soldier.

Robert Kerr on Dwight D Eisenhower

If you can't stand the heat, get out of the kitchen.

Harry S Truman

Half mad baronet, half beautiful woman.

R A Butler on Anthony Eden

The best prime minister we've got.

R A Butler on Anthony Eden. A reporter asked him: 'Mr Butler, would you say that he is the best prime minister we have?' All Butler could reply was 'Yes'.

Double-talk is his mother tongue.
Iain Macleod on Harold Wilson

A real centaur: part man, part horse's ass.
Dean Acheson on Lyndon B Johnson

He is an overripe banana, yellow outside, squishy in.
Reginald Paget on Anthony Eden at the time of the Suez Crisis

Aneurin Bevan: Where you born, laddie?
Harold Wilson: Yorkshiremen are not born – they are forged.
Bevan: I always knew there was something counterfeit about you.

He always looks as if he were on the verge of being found out.
Rebecca West on Harold Wilson

George Brown drunk is a better man than the prime minister [Harold Wilson] sober.
The Times

If one morning I walked on top of the water across the Potomac River, the headline that afternoon would read 'President Can't Swim'.

Lyndon B Johnson

Let's face it, Mr President. You're not a very likeable man.

Dean Acheson, when Lyndon B Johnson asked why he was not popular

I seldom think of politics more than 18 hours a day.

Lyndon B Johnson

He doesn't like cold intellectuals about him. He wants people who will cry when an old lady falls down in the street.

Jack Valenti on Lyndon B Johnson

Son, these are all my helicopters.

Lyndon B Johnson, to an officer who told him: 'Mr President, this is your helicopter'

Gerry Ford is so dumb, he can't fart and chew gum at the same time.

Lyndon B Johnson

Music means everything to me when I'm alone. And it's the best way of getting that bloody man Wilson out of my hair.

Edward Heath

If only he had lost his temper in public the way he does in private, he would have become a more commanding and successful national leader.

William Davis on Edward Heath

For years politicians have promised the moon. I'm the first one to deliver it.

Richard Nixon

You mustn't expect prime ministers to enjoy themselves. If they do, they mustn't show it – the population would be horrified.

Edward Heath

Action, not words.
The slogan of Edward Heath's unsuccessful 1966 general election campaign

---

Ted Heath disliked two things above all else: people who disagreed with him, and women. Margaret Thatcher was both.
Penny Junor

Edward Heath: Other countries have far greater problems than we have.
James Wellbeloved: No they haven't; we've got you.

He suffers from what you may regard as a fatal defect in a chancellor. He is always wrong.
Iain Macleod on James Callaghan

A lot of people are cleverer than I am, but I became prime minister and they didn't.
James Callaghan

As Moses, he would have mistimed his arrival at the parting of the waves.
Austin Mitchell on James Callaghan

He slaved like an indentured servant, and the public watched him sink in a morass of detail.
Hedrick Smith on Jimmy Carter's presidency

He has been perfecting the Teflon-coated presidency.

Patricia Schroeder on Ronald Reagan

He is the first man for 20 years to make the presidency a part-time job, a means of filling up a few of the otherwise blank days of retirement.

Simon Hoggart on Ronald Reagan

What did the President forget, and when did he forget it?

Adage on Reagan's involvement in the Iran–Contra affair, echoing the question concerning Nixon over Watergate: **'What did the President know, and when did he know it?'**

No shirt is too young to be stuffed.

Larry Zolf, on Canada's 40-year-old prime minister, Joe Clark

She has the eyes of Caligula, but the lips of Marilyn Monroe.

François Mitterrand on Margaret Thatcher

She is of such charming brutality.

Helmut Kohl on Margaret Thatcher

She cannot see an institution without hitting it with her handbag.

Julian Critchley on Margaret Thatcher

She has no imagination, and that means no compassion.

Michael Foot on Margaret Thatcher

She seemed to share the views so often expressed by party workers and, worse, to articulate them.

Julian Critchley on Margaret Thatcher

I often compare the prime minister with Florence Nightingale. She stalks through the wards of our hospitals as a lady with a lamp – unfortunately, it is a blowlamp.

Denis Healey on Margaret Thatcher

The prime minister says she has given the French president a piece of her mind – this is not a gift I would receive with alacrity.

Denis Healey on Margaret Thatcher

He can't help it. He was born with a silver foot in his mouth.

Ann Richards on George H W Bush

The boy who ran away from the circus to become an accountant.

Edward Pearce on John Major

It may be the cock that crows but it is the hen which lays the eggs.

Margaret Thatcher

A heady mixture of whisky and perfume.

Dr David Owen on Margaret Thatcher

I can't be grey and arrogant.

John Major

A man of gargantuan appetites and enormous drive, and not only in relation to women.

David Brock on Bill Clinton

The ideal [Conservative] leader should have the humility of Michael Howard, the charisma of Peter Lilley, the humour of John Redwood, the firmness of purpose of Stephen Dorrell, the family life of William Hague and the elegance of Kenneth Clarke.

Bryan Cassidy after John Major's defeat in 1997

In office, but not in power.

Norman Lamont on John Major, after being sacked as chancellor

He has achieved great things since 1997 but, paradoxically, he is in danger of destroying his legacy as he becomes increasingly obsessed by his place in history.

Clare Short on Tony Blair, in her resignation speech over the Iraq War

I'm sorry, we don't do God.

Alastair Campbell

If you said to me, name 25 million people who would maybe be president of the United States, he wouldn't have been in that category.
George W Bush's former business associate David Rubenstein

I'm proud of George. He's learned a lot about ranching since those first years when he tried to milk a horse. What's more, it was a male horse.
Laura Bush on her husband

Trump's face when he denounces White Nationalism and the KKK is the same face I made when my parents made me eat Brussels sprouts.
Brian O'Sullivan

He's the life and soul of the party, but he's not the man you want driving you home at the end of the evening.
Amber Rudd on Boris Johnson

It is my ambition and desire to so administer the affairs of the government while I remain President that if at the end I have lost every other friend on earth I shall at least have one friend remaining and that one shall be down inside me.
Abraham Lincoln

Being president is like being a jackass in a hailstorm. There's nothing to do but to stand there and take it.

Lyndon B Johnson

The Right Honourable Gentleman must not allow himself to be converted into an air raid shelter to keep the splinters from hitting his colleagues.

David Lloyd George, warning Winston Churchill not to weaken his own position by defending Neville Chamberlain's government. Spoken in the debate that led to the fall of that government and Churchill's emergence as prime minister

My esteem in this country has gone up considerably. Now when they wave to me, they use all their fingers.

Jimmy Carter

I want you to know that I am not going to make age an issue in this campaign. I am not going to exploit, for political purposes, my opponent's youth and inexperience.

Ronald Reagan

Being president is like running a cemetery: you've got a lot of people under you and nobody's listening.

Bill Clinton

There are some men who lift the age they inhabit, till all men walk upon higher ground in the lifetime.

Reference to George Washington in Maxwell Anderson's play *Valley Forge*

Like a plastic bag up a tree. No one knows how he got up there and no one can be bothered to get him down.

Bill Bailey on Ed Miliband

I prefer to be true to myself, even at the hazard of incurring the ridicule of others, rather than to be false, and to incur my own abhorrence.

Frederick Douglass

8

THE WORLD STAGE

**'Happily there seems to be no reason why we
should be anything more than spectators'**
Herbert Asquith as the First World War got
under way in the Balkans

At some point in your rise through the ranks, you will
face the issue of how far to stray from domestic politics.
At the top, you have no choice but to deal with Abroad.
And there are times when international relationships are
all-consuming. War is one of those times, as with the two
world wars, Korea, Suez, the Falklands, Iraq and, now,
the Ukraine War. Outside of armed conflict, Brexit and
our relationship with continental Europe dominated political life for four years, was a live issue for the previous
half-century and still lingers in the background.

Don't be tempted, therefore, by the insular cynicism
that 'foreigners don't vote'. In fact, it isn't even true; in
the UK, Commonwealth and Irish nationals can vote, as
can British nationals who have long been resident

overseas, and there are all kinds of complexities around dual nationals.

A more convincing truism is that 'all politics is local'. Many parliamentary candidates promote themselves through their local connections by upbringing or residence, whilst the parliamentary careers of others have been killed off by being exposed as a 'foreigner' from another town. MPs who appear to show more interest in foreign parts than their own constituencies will find themselves dubbed 'the Member for Islamabad East' or 'Jerusalem West' or 'Timbuktu', and extensive overseas travel will earn the nickname 'Marco Polo'. Norman Tebbit did not value Foreign Office experience: **'The Ministry of Agriculture looks after farmers and the Foreign Office looks after foreigners.'** That said, there are many ways in which the world stage can be a worthwhile platform.

WARRIOR POLITICIANS

'Patriotism is fundamentally a conviction that a particular country is the best in the world because you were born into it'
George Bernard Shaw

There are few stronger political lines than patriotism and few better opportunities to take them than in war. Some politicians made their reputation as successful war leaders (Churchill, Lloyd George, Thatcher). Others had their reputation seriously undermined by 'bad' wars (Blair, Eden). Neville Chamberlain is remembered for Munich and the unsuccessful appeasement of Hitler; Churchill described him as **'looking at foreign affairs through the wrong end of a municipal drainpipe'**.

There have been others whose own war service was a significant political asset. Harold Macmillan and Clement Attlee were amongst 264 MPs who fought in the First World War, of whom 22 died. Denis Healey, Edward Heath and Enoch Powell, amongst others, fought in the Second. In more recent times, Paddy Ashdown's military (and intelligence) career was a major political asset to him.

In the USA, one post-war president, Dwight D Eisenhower, was a military leader in the Second World War; Kennedy was a decorated war hero; Jimmy Carter had a naval career on nuclear submarines. Several others had problems explaining their 'draft dodging' from the Vietnam War – Bill Clinton and George W Bush – though Donald Trump made a virtue of it and said that those who died in war were 'losers' and 'suckers'. John Kerry campaigned for the Democratic nomination on the back of his Vietnam War record, but it backfired when one of his fellow veterans disputed his account of events.

BLESSED ARE THE PEACEMAKERS

'Meeting jaw-jaw is better than going to war-war'
Winston Churchill

The avoidance or conclusion of war is a less tangible and more elusive political achievement than victory on the battlefield. It is a struggle to find politicians whose careers were built on successful peacemaking: Woodrow Wilson's attempts to create a durable post-First World War architecture failed; Barack Obama's non-achievement was regretted even by the Nobel Committee, which had given him a prize. One Nobel Prize winner who devoted his life to peacekeeping and conflict resolution was Jimmy Carter, but after he retired from politics. Willy Brandt's *Ostpolitik* – of improving relations between West and East Germany in the 1970s – is perhaps the best example.

Post-war politicians in Britain have been distracted from the global stage by the need to adjust to Britain's own diminished economic and political standing. Harold Macmillan's 'Wind of Change' speech in 1960 was a crucial step in signalling a peaceful withdrawal from empire. Then there was Europe. Several major political careers were defined by joining the European Community that later evolved into the EU (Edward Heath), operating within it positively (Roy Jenkins) or sceptically (Margaret Thatcher), or leaving it (Cameron, Johnson, Farage). In parallel, there has been the increasingly one-sided 'special relationship' with the USA and the supposed personal chemistry between leaders: Macmillan and Kennedy; Thatcher and Reagan; Blair and George W Bush.

MAKING A SPLASH

'One third of the people of the world are asleep at any given moment. The other two thirds are awake and probably stirring up trouble somewhere'
Dean Rusk

You will, at some stage, be assailed by concerned constituents or refugee groups outraged by reports of some atrocity abroad. To please them, or because you care, you will stand up in Parliament and demand that 'something should be done'. The minister will agree but not do anything.

It is difficult today to imagine how William Gladstone, the Liberal leader, could have made speeches of up to five hours in Scottish towns to rapt audiences of thousands on such subjects as 'the Bulgarian atrocities' and the principles of foreign policy. The speeches helped to get him elected – for Midlothian – in 1880. Britain was then the largely undisputed superpower, so the views of its leaders mattered. The tradition of finger-wagging and moralising nonetheless continues. Simon Jenkins noted that **'the nagging desire to rule the world, or at least to tell it how to behave, is embedded in the genes of every British politician'**.

This 'nagging desire' is expressed in Parliament through numerous all-party groups covering almost every country in the world, from Albania and Azerbaijan to Western Sahara and Yemen. The political parties have the Friends of India/Pakistan/Israel or the Conservatives' Middle East Council. These groups provide extensive travel opportunities as well as immersion in foreign policy issues (and party fundraising opportunities).

Where there are large concentrations of ethnic minorities, the politics of their countries of origin loom large. This is most obviously true of the Indian subcontinent. A sizeable number of Labour MPs speak up for Pakistan, especially over Kashmir, and engage with issues of wider concern to Muslims, like Palestine. One consequence is that Hindu Indians and Jewish voters have been courted, successfully, by the Conservatives.

The spirit if not the substance of Gladstone is still alive in the wish of many British politicians to play a role 'calling out' human rights abuses from China to Zimbabwe, as well as demanding that Britain take a lead on climate change, humanitarian relief, global economic cooperation and much else. Acting on the world stage still has an irresistible appeal.

A diplomat is a person who can be disarming, even though his country isn't.
Adage

Diplomacy is the art of saying 'Nice doggie!' until you can find a rock.
Will Rogers

Diplomacy is to do and say
The nastiest thing in the nicest way.
Isaac Goldberg

English policy is to float lazily downstream, occasionally putting out a diplomatic boathook to avoid collisions.
Lord Salisbury

If you recognise anyone, it does not mean that you like him. We all, for instance, recognise the Right Honourable Gentleman the Member for Ebbw Vale [Aneurin Bevan].
Winston Churchill, on Britain's recognition of Communist China

---

England is nothing but the last ward of the European madhouse, and quite possibly it will prove to be the ward for particularly violent cases.
Leon Trotsky

Diplomacy is letting someone else have your way.
Lester B Pearson

A small acquaintance with history shows that all governments are selfish, and the French governments more selfish than most.
Lord Eccles

One cannot trust people whose cuisine is so bad ... The only thing they have ever done for European agriculture is mad cow disease ... After Finland, it is the country with the worst food.
The diatribe against Britain by President Jacques Chirac, which was credited with London securing the 2012 Olympics over Paris, with Finland's vote decisive.

We are not entitled to sell our friends and kinsmen down the river for a problematical and marginal advantage in selling washing machines in Dusseldorf.
Harold Wilson

Rolling on his back like a spaniel at any kind gesture from the French.
Harold Wilson on Edward Heath

The most mischievous and dangerous person alive.
Queen Victoria on Otto von Bismarck

This going into Europe will not turn out to be the thrilling mutual exchange supposed. It is more like nine middle-aged couples with failing marriages meeting in a darkened bedroom in a Brussels hotel for a group grope.

E P Thompson, 1975

Europe is not just about free trade and single currencies. It's about building a continent fit for Sir Edward Heath to conduct the European Community Youth Orchestra in the 'Ode to Joy'.

Mark Steyn

Europe depended on which leg – the left or the right – he put out of bed first.

Princess Lieven on Viscount Palmerston

To campaign against colonialism is like barking up a tree that has already been cut down.

Sir Andrew Cohen, 1958

THE SPECIAL RELATIONSHIP

The world must be made safe for democracy.
Woodrow Wilson

Americans will turn up six months late, and bomb the country next to where it is happening.
P J O'Rourke

War is God's way of teaching Americans geography.
Ambrose Bierce

Every time Europe looks across the Atlantic to see the American eagle, it observes only the rear end of an ostrich.
H G Wells

It is always best and safest to count on nothing from the Americans but words.
Neville Chamberlain

Scratch any American, and underneath you'll find an isolationist.
Dean Rusk

How can I talk to a fellow who thinks himself the first man in two thousand years to know anything about peace on earth?

Georges Clemenceau on Woodrow Wilson

What a woman!

Otto von Bismarck, after an audience with Queen Victoria

My good friends, for the second time in our history, a British prime minister has returned from Germany bringing peace with honour. I believe it is peace for our time. We thank you from the bottom of our hearts. Go home and get a nice quiet sleep.

Neville Chamberlain, 1938

We're eyeball to eyeball – and I think the other fellow just blinked.

Dean Rusk during the Cuban Missile Crisis

The world is getting so small that even the people in Java are our neighbours now.

Franklin D Roosevelt

It is far better to meet at the summit, rather than at the brink.

John F Kennedy

The only summit meeting that can succeed is one that does not take place.

Barry Goldwater

Oh, if the Queen were a man, she would like to go and give those horrid Russians whose word one cannot trust a beating.

Queen Victoria, letter to Benjamin Disraeli

The conference has lasted six weeks. It wasted six weeks. It lasted as long as a Carnival, and like a Carnival, it was an affair of masks and mystification. Our ministers went to it as men in distressed circumstances go to a place of amusement – to while away the time, with a consciousness of impending failure.

Benjamin Disraeli, 1864

War is the national industry of Prussia.

Honoré Gabriel Riqueti, comte de Mirabeau (attrib.)

If you're attacked, it's no longer a foreign war.

Franklin D Roosevelt

Time is the very material commodity which the Foreign Office is supposed to provide, in the same way as other departments provide other war materiel.

Robert Vansittart

To make a union with Britain would be fusion with a corpse.

Marshal Philippe Pétain

If Hitler invaded Hell, I would at least make a favourable reference to the Devil in the House of Commons.

Winston Churchill

They never pass up an opportunity to pass up an opportunity.

Attributed to Conor Cruise O'Brien about the Ulster Unionists, and Abba Eban about the Palestine Liberation Organization. Traceable back to George Bernard Shaw, of Lord Rosebery: **'He never missed an occasion to let slip an opportunity.'**

She would rather light candles than curse the darkness, and her glow has warmed the world.
Adlai Stevenson's eulogy for Eleanor Roosevelt

The wind of change is blowing through this continent [Africa], and, whether we like it or not, this growth of national consciousness is a political fact.
Harold Macmillan to the South African Parliament, 1960.
Not quite original, as in 1934 Stanley Baldwin said:
There is a wind of nationalism and freedom blowing round the world, and blowing as strongly in Asia as elsewhere.

I'd like that translated, if I may.
Harold Macmillan, after Nikita S Khrushchev took off his shoe and banged it on the table at the UN General Assembly, 1960

Story – probably fictitious – of George Brown, when foreign secretary, attending a function in Peru where he invited a woman to dance with him. She declined, on three grounds:
First, you are drunk. Second, this is the Peruvian national anthem. And third, I am the cardinal archbishop of Lima.

She probably thinks Sinai is the plural of sinus.

Jonathan Aitken on Margaret Thatcher

She will insist on treating other heads of government as if they were members of her Cabinet.

Ian Gilmour on Margaret Thatcher

I cannot forecast to you the action of Russia. It is a riddle wrapped in a mystery inside an enigma.

Winston Churchill

Russia and China are having their differences. But we cannot take too much comfort in the fact . . . They are simply arguing about what kind of shovel they should use to dig the grave of the United States.

Richard Nixon

A man I could do business with.
Margaret Thatcher on Mikhail Gorbachev. Unintentionally echoing Clement Attlee on Stalin:
He was clearly a pretty ruthless tyrant, but a man you could do business with because he said yes and no and didn't have to refer back. He was obviously the man who would make decisions, and he was obviously going to be difficult.

Overseas aid is the transfer of money from poor people in rich countries to rich people in poor countries.
Peter Bauer

I am a good friend to communists abroad, but I do not like them at home.
Cambodia's Prince Sihanouk

Defence policy? Well, until recently I did not know that you had one.
Australia's Sir Robert Menzies to Sir Stafford Cripps, 1936

Plasterass? I hope he hasn't got feet of clay, too.
Winston Churchill, on being told he was to meet Greece's General Plastiras

He is the only case I know of a bull who carries his own china with him.

Winston Churchill on John Foster Dulles

Great Britain has lost an empire, but not yet found a role.

Dean Acheson

For war to be just, three things are necessary: public authority, just cause, right motive.

St Thomas Aquinas

My foreign policy is to be able to take a ticket at Victoria Station and go anywhere I damn well please.

Ernest Bevin

Let us be masters of the Straits [of Dover] for six hours, and we shall be masters of the world.

Napoleon Bonaparte

The trouble with the French is they have no word for entrepreneur.

George W Bush to Tony Blair

A foreign secretary is always faced with this cruel dilemma. Nothing he can say can do very much good, and almost anything he may say may do a great deal of harm. Anything he says that is not obvious is dangerous; whatever is not trite is risky. He is forever posed between the cliché and the indiscretion.

Harold Macmillan

A good negotiation makes all parties uncomfortable.

John Kerry

Communiqués are like bikinis. What they reveal is alluring, but the essential points remain hidden.

Ambassador Karl-Günther von Hase

We've got an oven-ready Brexit deal. We just need to put it into the oven at gas mark 4, 20 minutes and Bob's your uncle.

Boris Johnson

The EU is failing, the EU is dying. I hope we have knocked the first brick out of the wall. I hope this is the first step towards a Europe of sovereign nation states trading together, neighbours together, friends together. But without the flags, anthems or useless old unelected presidents.

Nigel Farage, 23 June 2016

The British have chosen liberty with Brexit and can congratulate themselves.

Marine Le Pen

I deal with tough mathematical questions every day but please don't ask me to help with Brexit.

Stephen Hawking

We send the EU £350 million a week – let's fund the NHS instead.

Brexit battlebus

Nikita S. Khrushchev: Isn't it remarkable that you, a member of the ruling class, and I, from the working class, should control the two greatest socialist countries that ever existed?
Chou En-lai: Yes, and more remarkable still, each of us has betrayed the class from which he came.

A reputed exchange, quoted by Tony Benn

9
FIGHTING OFF CRITICISM

'"To hell with you". Offensive letter follows'
Correspondent of Sir Alec Douglas-Home

'It is better to have that fellow inside the tent pissing out than outside the tent pissing in'
Lyndon B Johnson on FBI director J. Edgar Hoover

You can expect to be criticised, often unfairly and nastily. You should heed Truman's adage: **'If you can't stand the heat, get out of the kitchen.'** And if you choose to stay in the kitchen and face the heat you will need to develop mechanisms to cope with criticism in all its forms, from heckling in public meetings, attacks in the print press and rude letters in green ink through to hostile trolling on social media.

THE TRADITION OF OFFENDING

'I always cheer up immensely if an attack is particularly wounding because I think, well, if they attack one personally, it means they have not a single political argument left'
Margaret Thatcher

'The longer you stay, you realise that sometimes you catch more flies with honey than with vinegar'
Strom Thurmond

Bevan described politics as a 'blood sport'. The essence of politics is that hunters use words to wound rather than dogs to kill.

There is a long-established tradition of heckling rudely at public meetings to throw the speaker off of their stride. Good public speakers have a repertoire of put-downs, usually involving colourful insults about the heckler's brain. Such as this, from Pierre Trudeau: **'The Honourable Gentleman disagrees; I can hear him shaking his head.'**

Parliament has a history of offensive, but witty, comments. Benjamin Disraeli was a master of the brutal put-down – like his dismissal of the Liberal leader, Lord John Russell: **'If a traveller were informed that such a man was the Leader of the House of Commons, he might begin to comprehend how the Egyptians** *worshipped an insect.'* Sir Geoffrey Howe is best remembered not for his economic policy but for Denis Healey's comment: **'Being attacked by the chancellor is like being savaged by a dead sheep.'**

The use of offensive humour has evolved from days when adversaries were prevented from crossing the aisle to throw punches or draw swords; hence the width between front benches of two swords' length. MPs are not allowed to use certain words like 'liar', which has led to a search for more convoluted and humorous – and potentially more wounding – insults. David Lloyd George said of Sir John Simon: **'The Right Honourable and Learned Gentleman has twice crossed the floor, each time leaving behind a trail of slime.'**

Until recently, the main critical battleground was the print press. Politicians still scour the broadsheets for serious analysis of their speeches and career prospects, and the tabloids to see if they have a splash. The fact that not all coverage is favourable will frequently lead to complaints of media bias. Don't go there. Some complaints are justified but, in general, complaints from politicians attract little sympathy. As Enoch Powell put it: **'For politicians to complain about the press is like fishermen complaining about the sea.'**

Moreover, the power of the print press has greatly diminished, especially amongst younger people who get their news online and form their opinions through social media. Over the last 20 years, the UK print press has lost two thirds of its readership. Like any aspiring politician, you have to learn how to use social media or, at least, live with it.

Social media have essentially imported three new elements into political communications. The first is speed. Events and other people's comments require an immediate response or the moment has passed. The demands of the 24-hour news cycle have intensified. Second, complex issues have been reduced to binary choices: like/dislike. And third, and most worryingly, there is anonymity, which provides trolls the opportunity to make hurtful and abusive comments to and about those in public life without providing an opportunity to respond.

Where issues have become very heated and controversial, the level of abuse has become extreme and violent. Women MPs in particular often receive threats of sexual violence and appear to be more exposed to abuse. Death threats are not uncommon. You may need to go to the police. Failing that, send out your tweets but don't read the replies.

The political master of social media was Donald Trump. Love him or hate him, he knew how to communicate. His clear, pungent, uncomplicated and often abusive Twitter account built him a following of almost 90 million at its peak at the end of 2019 from 3 million in 2015. He is eclipsed in sheer numbers of followers by Barack Obama, whose style is altogether more consensual and constructive, and whose following of 130 million exceeds pop stars like Justin Bieber and Rihanna. Not everyone is impressed by social media followership; some would even agree with David Cameron that **'too many tweets make a twat'**.

WHY POLITICIANS GET CRITICISED

You can't avoid criticism but you should try to avoid the particular faults unfortunately often associated with politicians. One is hypocrisy: the belief that politicians say one thing and do another, rarely practising what they preach. William Hague attacked the Blair government for hypocrisy: **'When we have a deputy prime minister who tells people not to drive and has two Jags himself, and where the minister who tells people not to have two homes turns out to have nine himself, no wonder the public believe politicians are hypocrites.'** The more recent Partygate scandal under Boris Johnson has hypocrisy at its core.

A second and common failing is the U-turn, especially when the U-turner shows no sign of contrition. Tony Benn attracted the wrath of Jimmy Reid, the union leader of the Clydeside shipbuilders: **'He has had more conversions on the road to Damascus than a Syrian long-distance lorry driver.'** John Maynard Keynes provided an escape route for politicians who reverse their judgements and policies: **'When the facts change, I change my mind.'** Frequently, however, it is not facts but political expediency which causes U-turns.

A further source of criticism is of politicians who insist on pursuing a vendetta or quarrel with a media critic and seem unable to draw a line under it. The good advice – variously attributed to Mark Twain, Abraham Lincoln and George Bernard Shaw, amongst others – for politicians who won't let go is: **'Don't get into a wrestling match with a pig. You both get dirty and the pig likes it.'**

Cruel criticism is often remembered long after the author's more constructive contributions are forgotten. I spent 20 years crafting serious but totally unmemorable interventions in Parliament. My only contribution to the repertoire of memorable remarks was a quote dreamt up in the morning before Prime Minister's Questions directed at Gordon Brown – a man who I liked and respected: **'The Prime Minister has gone from Stalin to Mr Bean; creating chaos out of order rather than order out of chaos.'**

*Far better to keep your mouth shut and let
everyone think you're stupid than to open it and
leave no doubt.*

Norman Tebbit to Dennis Skinner

---

*A putrefying albatross around the neck of this
government.*

Aneurin Bevan on Harold Macmillan's foreign secretary
Selwyn Lloyd

---

*I am not going to spend any time whatsoever
attacking the Foreign Secretary. Quite honestly,
I am beginning to feel extremely sorry for him. If
we complain about the tune, there is no reason to
attack the monkey when the organ grinder is
present.*

Aneurin Bevan, when Selwyn Lloyd replied to his
questions instead of Harold Macmillan

---

*Living proof that a pig's bladder on a stick can be
elected as a member of Parliament.*

Tony Banks on Terry Dicks

He stinks of money and insincerity.

Hugh Dalton on Sir Oswald Mosley, before he came out
as a Fascist

When they circumcised him, they threw away the wrong bit.

David Lloyd George (attrib.) on Herbert Samuel

There, but for the grace of God, goes God.

Winston Churchill on Sir Stafford Cripps

He will be as great a curse to this country in peace as he was a squalid nuisance in time of war.

Winston Churchill on Aneurin Bevan

If thy Nye offend thee, pluck it out.

Clement Attlee on Aneurin Bevan

Nye wasn't cut out to be a leader. He was cut out to be a prophet.

Richard Crossman on Aneurin Bevan

To hell with them. When history is written they will be the sons of bitches, not I.

Harry S Truman on his critics in the media

Labour MP in the Commons tea room: Nye is his own worst enemy.

Ernest Bevin: Not while I'm alive, he ain't.

It is better to be too clever by half than too stupid by three quarters.

Hugh Dalton to the young James Callaghan

He wouldn't go two rounds with a revolving door.

Vince Gair on Australian Liberal leader Billy Snedden

From Lord Hailsham we have had a virtuoso performance in the art of kicking a friend in the guts. When self-indulgence has reduced a man to the state of Lord Hailsham, sexual continence involves no more than a sense of the ridiculous.

Reginald Paget on Lord Hailsham's response to the Profumo affair

---

There are four ways of acquiring money: make it, earn it, marry it and borrow it. The Right Honourable Gentleman seems to know about all four.

Margaret Thatcher on the wealthy Labour Treasury minister Harold Lever

---

Like being flogged with a warm lettuce.

Paul Keating on an attack by John Hewson

When she goes to the dentist, he's the one who needs the anaesthetic.

Frank Dobson on Edwina Currie

Tomfool issues, barmy ideas, a kind of ageing, perennial youth who immatures with age.

Harold Wilson on Tony Benn

Yes, and tomorrow he is parachuting into Scotland to hold peace talks with the Duke of Hamilton.

Denis Healey, on being told of Tony Benn's 3.15am announcement that he was challenging him for Labour's deputy leadership; he was referring to the wartime arrival in Scotland of Hitler's deputy Rudolf Hess

---

He has something of the night about him.

Ann Widdecombe on her former Home Office boss Michael Howard

A bull in search of a china shop.

Unnamed union leader on Charles Clarke

He has crawled so far up the backside of NATO, you can't even see the soles of his feet.

Ken Livingstone on Gerald Kaufman

He has the face of a man who clubs baby seals.
Denis Healey on John Prescott

I remain to be convinced that Jacob Rees-Mogg has not at least considered ingesting his young.
James Felton

It wouldn't be spring, would it, without the occasional cuckoo.
Margaret Thatcher on criticism of her policies from the Bishop of Durham

The high priestess of fear.

Emmanuel Macron on Marine Le Pen

Putting Norman Tebbit in charge of industrial relations is like appointing Dracula to take charge of the blood transfusion service.
Eric Varley

Cecil Parkinson's red face looming over the despatch box is a pretty terrifying sight. I was not sure at one stage whether it was indignation, claret or a faulty sun lamp.
Peter Snape

She has done for our party what King Herod did for babysitting.

Andrew MacKay on Edwina Currie

It seems that during the previous debate I suggested the Right Honourable Lady [Barbara Castle] did not know what she was doing. I ask the House to consider what they would have thought of me if I had suggested that she did know what she was doing.

Iain Macleod, after being ordered to apologise to the House

Nicholas Soames [minister for food]: The British countryside is not set in aspic.
Tony Banks: You'd eat it if it was.

Labour MP: I can't vote tonight. I'm supposed to be in Crete.
Whip Walter Harrison: If you're not here at 10 tonight you'll be in concrete.

HECKLING

Churchill (on having a cabbage hurled at him):
I ask for the gentleman's ears, not his head.

Harold Wilson: Why do I stress the importance of the Royal Navy?
Heckler: Because you're in Chatham.

Heckler: I could swallow you in one bite.
Tommy Douglas: If you did, you'd have more brains in your belly than you have in your head.

Norman Tebbit to heckler: Calm down, my lad.
Heckler: You're not my dad.
Tebbit: I would quit while you're ahead, son. It's obvious I'm the only father you'll ever know.

Richard Nixon to heckler: The jawbone of an ass is just as dangerous today as it was in Samson's time.

MP: I will have you know, Sir, that I have asked no fewer than 97 parliamentary questions.
Heckler: Ignorant bastard!

Dan Quayle: Four more years!
Heckler: Four more months!

Heckler: Rubbish!

Harold Wilson: I'll come to your special interest in a minute, Sir.

Heckler: You are two-faced.

Geoffrey Dickens: Would I be wearing this face if I had two?

Heckler: I wouldn't vote for you if I were St Peter.

Sir Robert Menzies: If I were St Peter you wouldn't be in my constituency.

Heckler: Tell us what you know, Bob!

Menzies: I'll tell us what we both know. It won't take any longer.

Wendell Willkie: Now we are in Chicago . . .

Heckler: No you're not. You're in Cicero.

Willkie: Well, all right, this is Cicero. To hell with Chicago!

Speaker at a party conference: What do women in the Labour Party really want?

Heckler: Cut Neil Kinnock's balls off.

10

MISTAKES AND SURVIVING THEM

'The politician who didn't make a mistake is never a politician; and the politician who admitted them to you is never a politician'

John Major

'It depends on what the meaning of the word "is" is'

Bill Clinton

Your political career will start amidst optimism, hope and a belief that problems can be overcome. But you will make mistakes.

Governments make mistakes, and the issue arises as to who is to blame. Opposition parties make mistakes which contribute to election reverses. Individual politicians make mistakes: failures in relationships which can become a 'scandal'; bad decisions causing accidents which result in injury and death; errors in the handling of money. Failure isn't necessarily terminal: Churchill observed, **'Success is the ability to go from one failure to another with no loss of enthusiasm.'** Boris Johnson has turned that insight into a key guide to government.

How do politicians survive their mistakes? You can reduce the risk of making mistakes by avoiding making difficult decisions in the first place: finding the long grass into which to kick tricky questions. After the event, there are cover-ups, successful or otherwise. You can bury the bad news. You can try to shift the blame – up to bosses, down to subordinates, across to colleagues. There is distraction, sometimes known as 'the dead cat bounce'. There is outright denial. There are apologies: partial or comprehensive; sincere or false. You will soon learn how to save your political skin. How you deploy these techniques is down to how much you are a saint or a cynic at heart.

WHEN IS A MISTAKE A MISTAKE?

It isn't always obvious when a mistake has occurred. Bad decisions by government over, say, big transport or defence or power projects, leading to big delays, cost overruns or failing technology, may take years to be clearly identified, by which time the key decision makers have disappeared into retirement or another job. Recent mistakes would probably include Concorde, HS2, the civil nuclear power programme and the billions spent on NHS IT. The clarification only comes from an audit report or a public inquiry, which can take years. It may also be clear that a bad decision has been made, but only in hindsight; in real time, the decision may seem to have been justified based on facts known at the time.

The key point about political mistakes is that there is safety in numbers. If there are many fingerprints at the scene of the crime no individual can be held responsible. And with some of the most egregious mistakes, it is often genuinely difficult to pin down who made the crucial decisions since many agencies and individuals were involved at different stages or at different levels of administration. Also, a lot of bad mistakes are made due to 'group-think' and the failure of organisations to 'think outside the box' or to be prepared for the unexpected. The 2008 financial crisis had many authors in the banking system, the regulatory agencies and government. The security failures which led to 9/11; the lack of disaster preparation resulting in the havoc caused by Hurricane Katrina; the unravelling of the post-war occupation of Iraq; the chaotic withdrawal from Afghanistan – all fit that description. In government, as in war, victory, as John F Kennedy put it, *'has a thousand fathers; defeat is an orphan'*.

It is also sometimes a mistake to regard a 'mistake' as necessarily being a mistake. The politician who has a reputation for being 'gaffe prone' may simply be proving Alexander Chancellor's point that *'a common definition of a gaffe is when a politician tells the truth'*.

Or the politician may be indulging in excessive clarity, disregarding John Morley's warning that **'most mistakes in politics arise from flat and invincible disregard of the plain maxim that it is possible for the same thing to be and not to be'**.

There is also consolation to be had in the justified belief that the public, and its champions in the press, are simply unreasonable. As Ann Treneman put it: **'It is a peculiarity of our time that we want politicians to be human, and then, when they screw up, we demand that they be more professional.'**

MISTAKES AND APOLOGIES

There are two broad strategies for dealing with mistakes. The first is the orthodoxy of public relations: be honest, take responsibility, 'get it all out there', apologise, move on as quickly as possible. The second is to deny everything, refuse to accept responsibility, shift the blame and, above all, don't apologise.

There are many examples of the first, though the apology may not be all it seems. The objective is usually to try to draw a line under a damaging episode and hopefully to attract sympathy and understanding. Bill Clinton tried to conclude the Monica Lewinsky scandal, which led to a near-impeachment, by saying **'I've already said I made a bad mistake and it was indefensible.'** Tony Blair apologised for **'mistakes made'** in the invasion of Iraq and acknowledged that there were **'elements of truth'** in the claim that the

Islamic State terrorist group was energised by the invasion: a long way short of a full apology.

Boris Johnson twice apologised to Parliament over the breach of Covid rules in the Partygate affair without ever explicitly acknowledging his part in proceedings: *'I want to apologise. I know the rage they [the public] feel . . . There were things we simply didn't get right, and I must take responsibility.'* He expressed an apology whilst insisting that judgement on his own role must await an official inquiry (and then, a police investigation). He was also leaving open the possibility that his staff could be blamed and subject to disciplinary action without his paying any personal penalty.

A contrast can be made with the tradition, now seemingly dead, whereby ministers accepted responsibility for the mistakes of their department and resigned, even if they were not personally responsible. The last major case of such a resignation was Lord Carrington from the Foreign Office after the Argentine invasion of the Falklands. We now see such noble behaviour much as we see the Charge of the Light Brigade: brave but stupid.

There may, however, be good reasons to avoid direct self-incrimination: notably the risks in terms of legal action, both criminal and civil, when an aggrieved party can sue for damages. It is easier for the head of an organisation to apologise for something in which they were not personally implicated. David Cameron gave a fulsome apology – **'I am deeply sorry'** – for the events of Bloody Sunday in 1972 in Northern Ireland when 30 unarmed civilians were shot by British paratroopers, 13 fatally. The apology followed two major, protracted public inquiries and was given after prosecutions against individual soldiers were dropped.

It has become common for government to issue retrospective apologies for events in history for which perpetrators and victims are long dead, but which have continued symbolic significance: the longer ago the better. Theresa May made a statement expressing 'deep regret' for the 1919 Amritsar massacre of unarmed Sikhs by the British Army under the command of General Dyer. She was minus 38 years old at the time. The Canadian, Australian and New Zealand governments have expressed contrition for the maltreatment of indigenous people, Belgium for the brutal colonial exploitation of the Congo. Spain has, however, so far declined to respond to a Mexican demand to apologise for the near extermination of the Aztecs. No one has yet apologised for Roman atrocities, like Caesar's genocide of the Gauls. Even apologies for slavery and the slave trade have to be tempered with caution lest an admission of collective guilt could lead to demands for reparations.

Modern politicians fall well short of the humility of Henry IV of the Holy Roman Empire, who apologised to Pope Gregory VII by standing barefoot in the snow for three days seeking forgiveness for his military actions against the papacy. Indeed, there is a very robust approach to mistakes, exemplified by Donald Trump, of never apologising at all. Apologies and expressions of regret are seen as signs of weakness. Trump is familiar with legal action from his business days and learnt not to admit liability. He has shown, however regrettably, that bigger political dividends are often to be gained from attacking your accusers than standing barefoot in the snow waiting for forgiveness.

If you make a bad mistake but lack the confidence and bluster of a Donald Trump and cannot face eating humble pie, there is the option of procrastination and evasion, 'sweeping it under the carpet'. There are well-developed techniques for making this happen. One is to announce an investigation or official inquiry with some fanfare but imprecise terms of reference, conducted by someone unlikely to rock the boat. This will ideally take a long time to start and will be finished long after you have moved on. Or, if there is no alternative to making public some embarrassing information, make sure that it leaks out when there is something else dominating the news: **'a good day to bury bad news'**, as spin doctor Jo Moore emailed to colleagues on 9/11. Another technique is to create a distraction: the 'dead cat bounce'. A classic case was Boris Johnson's attempt to distract from Partygate by attacking Labour leader Keir Starmer for a failure to prosecute Jimmy Savile, the notorious paedophile. The fact that the accusations were both irrelevant and wrong was beside the point.

It is a normal human instinct to cover up mistakes. And government ministers and other politicians are only human. Unless exposed by the press, parliamentary questioning or hunters for information, many mistakes are hidden. It has become an orthodoxy that politicians are damaged more by cover-ups than the original fault; Watergate was the classic case. But the proposition is difficult to prove since, if there are other, more successful cover-ups, we will never know about them.

She gave me a look only a mother could give a child.
George W Bush on Queen Elizabeth II, after he had mistakenly referred to her having visited the White House in 1776, not 1976

Sometimes I despair for that son of mine.
George H W Bush on George W Bush in an aside to a US senator

Oh dear, I hope it wasn't anybody important.
Queen Elizabeth II to Clare Short, after her mobile phone went off during a Privy Council meeting

An inverted pyramid of piffle.
Boris Johnson, dismissing (true) accusations about his private life

I have made my mistakes, but in all my years in public life I have never profited, never profited from public service – I have earned every cent. And in all my years of public life, I have never obstructed justice. And I think, too, that I could say that in my years of public life, that I welcome this kind of examination, because people have got to know whether or not their president is a crook. Well, I am not a crook.
Richard Nixon during Watergate

We may make mistakes at the beginning and shoot the wrong people, but there are many things worse than bloodshed, and slavery is one of them.

The Irish revolutionary Padraig Pearse, before his execution for taking part in the Easter Rising

---

There are three bodies no sensible man directly challenges: the Roman Catholic Church, the Brigade of Guards and the National Union of Mineworkers.

Harold Macmillan

The commonest error in politics is sticking to the carcass of dead policies.

Lord Salisbury

I should be pleased, I suppose, that Hitler has carried out a revolution on our lines. But they are Germans, so they will end by ruining our idea.

Benito Mussolini

[My daughter] Caroline is a cute kid, but we shouldn't let her plan any more invasions.

John F Kennedy after the fiasco of the Bay of Pigs

Good God! That's done it. He's lost us the tarts' vote.

The Duke of Devonshire, on hearing Stanley Baldwin accuse the press lords Rothermere and Beaverbrook of exercising **'power without responsibility: the prerogative of the harlot throughout the ages'**

There was no impropriety whatsoever in my acquaintance with Miss Keeler ... I shall not hesitate to issue writs for libel and slander if scandalous allegations are made or repeated outside this House.

John Profumo

From now on, the pound abroad is worth 14 per cent or so less in terms of other currencies. It does not mean, of course, that the pound here in Britain in your pocket or in your purse or in your bank has been devalued.

Harold Wilson, 1967

The wife don't like her hair blown about.

John Prescott, explaining why he was driven 250 yards to the party conference in Bournemouth

---

I've looked on many women with lust. I've committed adultery in my heart many times. God knows I will do this and forgives me.

Jimmy Carter, in an interview with *Playboy* one month prior to the 1976 election

It could have been spinach dip or something.

Monica Lewinsky in her grand jury testimony, on the semen stain on her infamous blue dress

I did not have sexual relations with that woman . . . Miss Lewinsky.

Bill Clinton

In my country, first we go to jail and then we become president.

Nelson Mandela to Bill Clinton

I think that gay marriage should be between a man and a woman.

Arnold Schwarzenegger

Stand up, Chuck, let 'em see ya.
Joe Biden, to Missouri state senator Chuck Graham, who
was in a wheelchair

Why did nobody notice it?
Queen Elizabeth II to Professor Luis Garicano, apropos
economists' failure to spot the global crash of 2008

**A woman who always keeps her promises has
called an election she promised not to, in order to
obtain a mandate she already has, for a policy she
said was a bad idea.**
David Robjant, letter to the *Guardian* regarding Theresa
May calling the 2017 election to get Brexit through

**Had this weird dream Theresa May humiliated
herself in snap election and clung to power
with homophobe fundamentalist terrorist
sympathisers.**
Tweet from Owen Jones after Theresa May struck a deal
with Northern Ireland's Democratic Unionists to stay in
office

**These, they're dangerous. They trap you, especially
those furry ones. It's the furry guys that get you in
real trouble.**
George H W Bush on the hazards of roving microphones

I crashed the car in the ditch.

Boris Johnson to the 1922 Committee on his handling of
the Owen Paterson affair

**There's a general whiff of 'we are the masters now'
about their behaviour. It has to stop, it has to stop
soon. It seems to me, as a lifelong Conservative, that
much of what they are doing is un-Conservative in
its behaviour. This government has done a number
of things that have concerned me deeply: they have
broken the law, the illegal prorogation of Parliament.
They have broken treaties, I have in mind the
Northern Ireland Protocol. They have broken their
word on many occasions.**

John Major on Boris Johnson's government

**People will forgive a politician they love almost any
sin . . . as long as the peccadillo is not flaunted.**

Theodore H White

**I have never had a great many baths myself.
It does not make a great deal of difference to your
health if you have fewer.**

Minister of Fuel Hugh Gaitskell urging the public to save
energy during the fuel crisis of 1947

Now we've all been screwed by the Cabinet.
The *Sun*'s headline the morning after Black Wednesday, 1992, and in the wake of revelations of sleaze

Was this really the operation I had voted for? Did I really think, when the House of Commons voted to support the American action, that it would be carried out with such boneheaded stupidity?
Boris Johnson, 2004, on the US's administration of occupied Iraq

I was told as a young man that the two occupational hazards of the House of Commons were alcohol and adultery. The huroosh that follows the intermittent revelations of the sexual goings-on of an unlucky MP has convinced us that the only safe pleasure for a parliamentarian is a bag of sweets.
Julian Critchley

There's a lot we need to do in this party of ours. Our base is too narrow and so, occasionally, are our sympathies. You know what some people call us: the Nasty Party. Twice we went to the country unchanged, unrepentant, just plain unattractive. And twice we got slaughtered.
Theresa May

I have made mistakes, but I was only trying to protect my family . . . I am not Superwoman. The reality of my daily life is that I'm juggling a lot of balls in the air. Sometimes some of the balls get dropped.

Cherie Blair, on her involvement with Peter Foster, who was known by everyone other than herself to have a criminal record for fraud

***

A gaffe is accidental. Mine never are. I like to shock, and I do it deliberately.

Alan Clark

***

Every so often, John [Major] and I will be sitting in Number 10 talking about how things are going, and a private secretary comes in and says, 'Prime Minister, there's something else we think you should know.' We know what's coming, and it's got to the point where we just look at each other and burst out laughing.

Ken Clarke to Nick Comfort at the height of one outbreak of Tory 'sleaze'

***

This is the operative statement. The others are inoperative.

Richard Nixon's press secretary Ron Ziegler, conceding for the first time that the White House had been involved in Watergate

No favours, but slightly quicker.

The five words in an email that triggered the resignation of David Blunkett as home secretary. It concerned the speeding-up of a visa application for the nanny of his former lover

We are going to win – maybe by 70–30.
David Cameron, prior to the Brexit referendum

Whether we like it or not, there are moments in history when pessimism is the appropriate response.
David Olusoga

11

FAILURE, DECLINE, DEFEAT AND ESCAPE

'A halo only has to slip nine inches and it becomes a noose'
Iain Macleod

'In war you can only be killed once, but in politics many times'
Winston Churchill

I didn't want to discourage you earlier, but honesty compels me to point out that you might finish your time in politics as living proof of Enoch Powell's gloomy epitaph that **'all political careers end in failure'**. I believe he exaggerates, since some politicians have a legacy of achievement in office and a record of success at the ballot box, and leave public life enjoying respect, even

affection. Many others, however, taste demotion, humiliation and defeat. You have been warned.

DEFEAT

'The people have spoken, the bastards'
Wendell Willkie

For every election winner, there is a loser (usually several).
Those MPs who achieve praise and fame by winning a
marginal seat can find themselves at highest risk of losing
next time round. Other MPs who have given years of
dedicated service as constituency members may be swept
away in a political tsunami, as happened to many Conservative MPs in 1997, Scottish Labour and Lib Dems in
2015, and 'red wall' Labour MPs in 2019.

Defeat for an incumbent MP (or, for that matter,
local councillor) can be traumatic. It isn't just the loss of a
job; many others have faced and coped with redundancy.
There is also the responsibility for others, members of
the MP's constituency and parliamentary staff, who have
been made unemployed too. Crucially, there is the sense
of rejection by the local community, where the MP and
their family probably live. There is public humiliation
and embarrassment, with jeering, crowing opponents
and news reporters who smell blood. There is anger and
recrimination over mistakes made by the party's high
command or locally, or over low blows landed by the
opposition.

I write from experience. The satisfaction of winning four times was then more than cancelled out by the experience of losing. The pain of losing was eased only by the knowledge that most of my party colleagues had gone down together and by being defeated by a decent and likeable opponent in my constituency. Eventually, two years later, I got my revenge, winning the seat back.

For party leaders, defeat can be terminal. Modern Conservative leaders are rarely allowed a second try. William Hague and Iain Duncan Smith were despatched quickly, though both returned later as ministers. Theresa May did not long survive her botched campaign in 2017. Labour has been more indulgent. Gaitskell, Kinnock and Corbyn all had two defeats to their name. My party, the Liberal Democrats, had five leaders in five years (including two years of me), reflecting frustration over three bad elections.

Other democracies treat losers more gently. Most defeated US presidential candidates return to be state governors or senators and some retain great political influence (Goldwater as a conservative ideologue; Al Gore, as a climate change campaigner; Trump, as Trump). Earlier defeated candidates include Thomas Jefferson, Theodore Roosevelt and (three-time loser) William Jennings Bryan, whose legacy is one of the greatest pieces of political oratory in history when, at the 1896 Democratic convention, he attacked the gold standard: *'You shall not crucify mankind upon a cross of gold.'* Even such an inauspicious role as defeated vice-presidential candidate can lead to great things. Thomas Dewey's 1948 running mate was Earl Warren, who after returning to his role as governor of California, became the fourteenth chief justice of the Supreme Court, one of the most influential jurists in US history.

DEMOTION

The laws of political as well as physical gravity dictate that what goes up also comes down. Thomas Paine observed of Edmund Burke: *'He rose like a rocket and fell like a stick.'* Demotion can be very hurtful. Barbara Castle bitterly observed: *'I have been discarded like a piece of old junk.'*

There could be several reasons for demotion. Some ministers gain a reputation – fairly or not – for being incompetent, ineffective or just unlucky. Recent examples include Chris Grayling in various roles and Gavin Williamson at the Department for Education. Newspaper sketch writers lampoon them; opposition MPs ridicule them and eventually they are demoted or sacked to ease government embarrassment or to put them out of their misery. Then there are the rivals or plotters or ideological opponents who the prime minister has decided are more trouble inside the tent than out of it. Margaret Thatcher gradually got rid of the 'wets' in her Cabinet and replaced them with 'true believers'. Tony Blair tried to build up the 'Blairite' rather than 'Brownite' tendency in his government. Boris Johnson has ruthlessly excluded Remainers and known opponents.

Then there are those who can be jettisoned without too much fuss to 'refresh' the Cabinet – to admit more women or younger people to improve the 'look' – or because they have no independent power base to mobilise in their defence. Prime ministers who are in a political hole will often try to restore authority by sweeping Cabinet changes, sacrificing friends and foes alike. Harold Macmillan was accused by Jeremy Thorpe of demonstrating that **'no man has greater love than that he lays down his friends for his life'**. The process of demoting colleagues, including friends and allies, is one of the sternest tests of political leadership. It is a process greatly eased if the pill of demotion can be sweetened with an important-sounding, if in fact less important, role. The leader of the House of Commons is one of those career cushions, along with offers of peerages, knighthoods, select committee chairs or a roving ambassadorship.

HANGING IN AND HANGING ON

'I have seen a great many men in public life, and one of their besetting sins is to stay in office too long'
Harry S Truman

For those who are on the way down, there is a comfortable resting place. Being an MP is, after all, a pleasant enough existence for someone with a 'safe' seat. Those who are active can build a reputation as the voice of experience and accumulated wisdom. When Ken Clarke left the government, he progressed, as the longest serving member of Parliament, to become the Father of the House which, under House protocol, gave him a guaranteed speaking slot on big occasions, which he used to great effect during the fraught Brexit negotiations. Edward Heath had the same position, which he used to settle scores with Margaret Thatcher. Since her defenestration as party leader, Theresa May has remained a brooding presence on the backbenches, with penetrating, well-timed, well-publicised barbs aimed at her successor.

Until recently, a base in Parliament for an ex-minister or party grandee could be used to leverage substantial outside earnings. The experience of Owen Paterson, a former Cabinet minister, may, however, have put a dampener on such activities as parliamentary lobbying and 'consultancy'. Having been heavily criticised by the parliamentary standards commissioner, and following a botched effort to change the rules to save him, he felt obliged to resign. The Conservatives then lost to the Liberal Democrats in the ensuing North Shropshire by-election.

All MPs must make a calculation as to when to leave the stage with a good reputation, accepting that they will be missing the fun. Some get the timing wrong. Dennis Skinner made a big reputation as the Beast of Bolsover, an ex-miner and champion of 'old Labour', whose loud, disrespectful interventions in Parliament terrorised nervous ministers, Tory and New Labour alike. Instead of leaving with his reputation intact, he could not resist standing one more time in 2019, aged 87, in order to be Father of the House, only to be defeated by a Conservative.

The people have spoken. It's just going to take a little time to figure out exactly what they said.

Bill Clinton, on the cliffhanger result of the election of his successor

---

I lost my election because of my campaign, not because of what anyone else did.

Mitt Romney

I don't mind not being president. I just mind that somebody else is.

Ted Kennedy after being defeated for the Democratic nomination

---

I was reminded of a story that a fellow-townsman of ours used to tell – Abraham Lincoln. They asked him how he felt once after an unsuccessful election. He said he felt like a little boy who had stubbed his toe in the dark. He said that he was too old to cry, but it hurt too much to laugh.

Adlai Stevenson conceding defeat to Dwight D Eisenhower

At about 11.30 on election night, they just push you off the edge of the cliff – and that's it. You might scream on the way down, but you're going to hit the bottom and you're not going to be in office.

Walter Mondale

It's amazing. You cross the big hurdles, and when you get to the small ones you get tripped.

Albert Reynolds

As a final indignity for the defeated warrior, Vice President Nixon had to preside over the roll call of the Electoral College. 'This is the first time in 100 years that a candidate for the presidency announced the result of an election in which he was defeated,' he told the assembled members of Congress. 'I do not think we could have a more striking and eloquent example of the stability of our constitutional system.' He got a standing ovation.

Nancy Gibbs

Politics is a funny game. One day you're a rooster, the next a feather duster.

Fred Daly

As I leave you I want you to know – just think how much you're going to be missing. You won't have Nixon to kick around anymore, because, gentlemen, this is my last press conference.

Richard Nixon, after losing the California gubernatorial election

---

I gave them a sword. And they stuck it in and they twisted it with relish. And I guess if I'd been in their position I'd have done the same thing.

Richard Nixon to David Frost

Tell him he's no longer president.

Advice given to the butler of Charles Evans Hughes, who went to bed mistakenly thinking he had defeated Woodrow Wilson in 1916

My unhappy constituents did not want 'safety'. That meant the dole. They wanted work. So they very properly voted me out.

Harold Macmillan

I feel I have had a very interesting life, but I am rather hoping there is still more to come. I still haven't captained the England cricket team or sung at Carnegie Hall.

Jeffrey Archer

Dear Chief Secretary, I'm afraid there is no money. Kind regards – and good luck! Liam.

Note left by the outgoing Labour chief secretary, Liam Byrne, for his Lib Dem successor, David Laws, 2010

I have never pretended to be the greatest House of Commons man but I can pay the house the greatest compliment I can by saying that from the first until the last I have never stopped fearing it. The tingling apprehension I felt at three minutes to 12 today I felt as much ten years ago and every bit as acute. It is in that fear that respect is retained. I wish everyone, friend or foe, well and that's that, the end.

Tony Blair

There is only one thing worse than the first term in opposition, and that's the second.

John Howard

I will shortly leave the job that it has been the honour of my life to hold ... I do so with no ill will, but with enormous and enduring gratitude to have had the opportunity to serve the country I love.

Theresa May

The Tory party ran screaming from side to side of the sinking ship before tossing Harold Macmillan over the side in an act of propitiation.

Julian Critchley

A statesman is judged by results. If his policy fails, he goes. It may be unfair, but there is a kind of rough justice about it.

Robert Boothby

You have sat too long for any good you have been doing. Depart, I say, and let us have done with you. In the name of God, go!

Oliver Cromwell, forcibly dissolving the Rump Parliament, 1653. Repeated by Leo Amery to Neville Chamberlain, 1940 and David Davis to Boris Johnson, 2022

We have been borne down in a torrent of gin and beer.

William Gladstone on the Liberals' defeat in the 1874 election

---

The cabin boys have taken over the ship.

Lord Beaverbrook on the meeting of dissident Tory MPs that ended Lloyd George's coalition government and was perpetuated in the 1922 Committee

If this is a blessing, it is certainly very well disguised.

Winston Churchill to his wife, after losing the 1945 election

During the past few weeks I felt sometimes that the Suez Canal was flowing through my room.

Lady Clarissa Eden

If you're not made Pope in the Roman Catholic Church, you can still be a perfectly good Cardinal Archbishop of Milan.

R A Butler, after failing to become prime minister

The prime minister has to be a butcher, and know the joints. That is perhaps where I have not been quite competent, in knowing the ways you can cut up a carcass.

R A Butler

I could not accept the Order of the Garter from my sovereign, when I had received the Order of the Boot from the people.

Winston Churchill, subsequently

There are two supreme pleasures in life. One is ideal, the other real. The ideal is when a man receives the seals of office from his Sovereign. The real pleasure comes when he hands them back.

Lord Rosebery

You can always get the truth from an American statesman after he has turned 70, or given up all hope of the presidency.

Wendell Phillips

As long as the old firm was Townshend and Walpole, the utmost harmony prevailed, but it no sooner became Walpole and Townshend than things went wrong.

Sir Robert Walpole

All political lives, unless they are cut off in mid-stream at a happy juncture, end in failure, because that is the nature of politics and of human affairs.

Enoch Powell

My great concern is not whether you have failed, but whether you are content with failure.

Abraham Lincoln

The great art of governing consists of not letting men grow old in their jobs.

Napoleon Bonaparte

The fall of Parnell left Ireland with a dead god instead of a leader.

G M Young

As I sat opposite the Treasury bench, the ministers reminded me of one of those marine landscapes not very unusual on the coast of South America. You behold a range of exhausted volcanoes, not a flame flickers on a single pallid crest, but the situation is still dangerous. There are occasional earthquakes, and ever and anon the dark rumbling of the sea.

Benjamin Disraeli on Gladstone's Liberal government

Gladstone . . . spent his declining years trying to answer the Irish Question; unfortunately whenever he was getting warm, the Irish secretly changed the question.

W C Sellar and R J Yeatman, *1066 and All That*

Gladstone, when asked in extreme old age why he had clung to public office for so long, replied in surprise: 'Why, don't you know? To keep Mr [Joseph] Chamberlain out, of course.'

Richard Jay, *Joseph Chamberlain: A Political Study*

Sit down, man. You're a bloody tragedy.

James Maxton to Ramsay MacDonald during his last Commons speech (attrib.)

Hawking his conscience around from conference to conference, asking to be told what to do with it.

Ernest Bevin's assessment of Labour's pacifist leader George Lansbury, shortly before his removal in 1936

Churchill: A Study in Failure

Robert Rhodes James's biography, covering the years 1900–1939

Dewey defeats Truman.
Erroneous headline carried by first editions of the *Chicago Tribune*, 1948

Well, he seemed such a nice old gentleman, I thought I would give him my autograph as a souvenir.
Adolf Hitler on Neville Chamberlain, after the Munich Conference

---

I fired him because he wouldn't respect the authority of the president. I didn't fire him because he was a dumb son of a bitch, although he was, but that's not against the law for generals. If it was, half to three quarters of them would be in jail.
Harry S Truman after firing General Douglas MacArthur

**'. . . let him never come back to us!
There would be doubt, hesitation and pain.
Forced praise on our part, the glimmer of twilight,
Never glad confident morning again.'**
Nigel Birch, quoting Robert Browning to Harold Macmillan in calling for his departure after the Profumo affair

---

I am Al Gore, and I used to be the next president of the United States.
Al Gore, addressing an audience of students

It is not so much power that corrupts; it is the withdrawal of power that pains.

Lord Rawlinson, on Margaret Thatcher's attacks on Europe after being forced from office

It's no good sulking in your tent like Ted Heath. That's really appalling.

Denis Healey, unexpectedly defeated by Michael Foot for the Labour leadership

There comes a time in every man's life when he must make way for an older man.

Reginald Maudling, on Margaret Thatcher replacing him as shadow foreign secretary with John Davies, one year his senior

Margaret Thatcher and Ted Heath both have a great vision. The difference is that Margaret Thatcher has a vision that Britain will one day be great again, and Ted Heath has a vision that Ted Heath will one day be great again.

Robert Jones

Like most people, I couldn't care who he goes to bed with, as long as it isn't me.

Ken Livingstone on David Mellor

The President of the Commission, Mr Delors, said at a press conference the other day that he wanted the European Parliament to be the democratic body of the Community. He wanted the Commission to be the executive, and wanted the Council of Ministers to be the Senate. No! No! No!

The comments by Margaret Thatcher that triggered the resignation of Sir Geoffrey Howe and led ultimately to her removal

---

It's a funny old world.

Margaret Thatcher on her removal

The longest suicide note in history.

Gerald Kaufman on Labour's 1983 election manifesto

I don't want to spend more time with my family.

Nicholas Ridley, facing demands for his resignation, 1990

It was certainly rich of [David] Mellor to warn the press it was drinking in the Last Chance saloon, while all the time he was playing the piano in the bordello next door.

Sun

He is departing to spend more time with his lawyers.

Brian Wilson on Jonathan Aitken's resignation as chief secretary to pursue a libel action against the *Guardian*. It culminated in his imprisonment for perjury

---

It's a fairly unique position; to have been in charge of prison funding and then to have been an inmate. I wish I'd been more generous.

Jonathan Aitken

Few things reveal more about political leaders and their systems than the manner of their downfall.

Antony Beevor

From triumph to downfall is but a step. I have seen a trifle decide the most important issues in the gravest affairs.

Napoleon Bonaparte

The sky is darkening with the wings of chickens coming home to roost.

Lord Callaghan on Black Wednesday, 1992

There is a very big difference. I lead my party – he follows his.

Tony Blair on John Major

My advice is to quit when you're behind.
Tony Blair to William Hague

You were the future once.
David Cameron to Tony Blair

He has the judgement of King Lear, the decisiveness of Hamlet, the paranoia of Othello and the loyalty of Brutus. But at least we've got rid of Lady Macbeth.
Bob Marshall-Andrews on Gordon Brown after he succeeded Tony Blair

For the last years of his life, he was only a melancholy passenger in the Conservative ship.
Clement Attlee on Ramsay MacDonald

Lose. Lose. Lose. Lose. Blair. Blair. Blair. Lose. Lose. Lose. Lose.
Lord Mandelson, making a point about Labour's performance in the 11 most recent general elections

12

RETIREMENT

'I was my best successor, but I decided not to succeed myself'

Pierre Trudeau

To go or not to go? One of the most difficult decisions you will have to make is when to step down, to leave the stage. Politics is one of the few professions without an upper age limit.

WHY RETIRE?

'Pain is temporary. Quitting lasts for ever'

Lance Armstrong

Most of us flatter ourselves with the idea that we are indispensable. That may be even more true of politicians, whose careers demand resilience, stamina and a capacity for self-promotion more than most. A selfish wish to cling to power and its trappings may be augmented by an unselfish wish to complete a job or a belief that there is more to give. There may be more complex political motivation, such as fear that an opposing party or an enemy might fill the vacancy or a wish to protect one's party from an unwanted by-election. Unpopular leaders can be unifiers. It was said of Iain Duncan Smith: **'At least under IDS we were all united in trying to get rid of him.'**

In authoritarian states, ageing dictators cling to power in part because they fear retribution from those they have persecuted or their families, or having corruption exposed. Robert Mugabe had to be forced out of the presidency of Zimbabwe, aged 93. In Malawi, Hastings Banda was 'president for life' before being defeated in a democratic election aged 96. Democracies have few comparable figures, though in Malaysia, Mahathir bin Mohamad briefly returned from retirement to be prime minister aged 94. The United States has a crop of powerful politicians all well into their seventies: President Biden, Donald Trump; or even eighties: Mitch McConnell, Nancy Pelosi, Bernie Sanders.

The public appears to have mixed views about older political leaders, valuing wisdom and experience but recognising that politicians, like everyone else, experience a decline in cognitive functions and become set in their prejudices and habits. A recent US survey suggested that, if public preferences were respected, 70 per cent of senators would retire on grounds of age.

But public attitudes are shaped by the particular rather than the general. In the USA, one of the most popular modern presidents was Ronald Reagan, who assumed his eight-year presidency a few days short of his seventieth birthday. In 2019, when the two US presidential candidates were well over 70, age was not a determining factor and both are now holding out the possibility of running again and governing in their eighties. Britain has had leaders of an advanced age but they were unique, iconic figures: Churchill was prime minister until 80 (much to the frustration of his heir apparent, Anthony Eden); Gladstone embarked on his fourth ministry aged 84.

THE EXIT DOOR

'Mr Gladstone has gone out – disappeared all in a moment'
Queen Victoria, gleefully

There is no established ritual for political retirement, no gold watch at 65. Some British leaders have had to be dragged kicking and screaming by their Cabinet colleagues to accept that they could not go on, most notably Margaret Thatcher. Some resigned mysteriously, like Harold Wilson, the reason apparently being mental and physical health, including a diagnosis of early onset dementia. Some lost the confidence of their party in Parliament (Heath, May). Tony Blair left apparently on his own terms and with the unusual accolade of a standing ovation in the Commons, but his resignation followed years of wrangling with Gordon Brown over the succession. Some countries have been far less indulgent of leaders who overstayed their welcome. Following the long premiership of John Howard, Australia had seven prime ministers in ten years as coup followed coup in both major parties.

At a leadership level, the issue is often one of balancing a self-assessment of one's ability to do the job against others' verdict on one's continuing political appeal. The dilemma was posed by Tony Blair: **'You start at your most popular and least capable and you end at your most capable and least popular.'**

At a less elevated political level, most MPs have to make a private calculation as to how to leave 'on a high' if possible, or with at least some basic dignity. And that, in turn, depends on what comes next.

AFTER RETIREMENT

'The House of Lords is like heaven – you want to go there some day, but not while there is any life left in you'
Lord Denning

There is an adage that **'there is nothing quite as ex as an ex-MP'**. The retiree may have a reputation, good or bad, but no longer has the influence and prestige, such as it is, of a serving parliamentarian, nor the sense of validation which comes from having been elected by one's fellow citizens. Especially for those who have left, defeated, there are reports from the former members' organisation of rejection, isolation and mental illness. Few are greatly comforted by having the opportunity 'to spend more time with their families.'

One long-established retirement route was via the House of Lords. But that route is now largely closed to opposition members or even to government supporters who are politically out of favour. And the award of peerages to large numbers of non-politicians in return for party donations or other party service has devalued the institution. Some recent party leaders and senior politicians accepted peerages after leaving the Commons (Wilson, Callaghan, Thatcher, Heseltine, Ashdown, Hague), whilst others have declined or not been offered one (Major, Blair, Brown, Cameron, Osborne, Clegg, Corbyn). Critics of the Lords, like Labour MP Austin Mitchell, for example, can be brutal: **'An ermine-lined dustbin, an up-market geriatric home with a faint smell of urine.'**

A tricky issue for retirees is money. Parliamentary pensions, especially for ex-ministers, are generous by most standards. But senior politicians can earn large sums after retirement. There are very generous speaking fees, for one. It was reported that Tony Blair was paid £300,000 to £400,000 for big engagements. For recent ex-ministers with good reputations, fees range from £8,000 to £10,000. There are also royalties from books: David Cameron was reputed to have been paid an advance of £800,000 to write his, Boris Johnson more.

There will also be offers to sit on the boards of companies with remuneration attached. Politicians may believe that this is a compliment on their abilities, but the motivation is usually to get access to their decision-making contacts. John Major caused controversy by chairing the private equity group Carlyle. David Cameron caused even more controversy by teaming up with Lex Greensill and engaging in lobbying government departments on his behalf. It was reported that he had made £60 million from a share listing and £1 million a year for 25 days a year of work. Nick Clegg provides one of the most successful, if controversial, examples of a successful shift to a business career, having become one of the top executives of one of the world's biggest companies: Facebook, now Meta.

Most politicians, however, don't enter politics to make money. If that was the motivation, they would have gone into business full time. The ideal position for most ex-politicians is still to have influence in the wider political debate. Michael Heseltine and John Major have emerged from retirement to be significant Conservative influencers on the debates on Brexit and on the future of the Tory Party; Tony Blair on the Labour side. Gordon Brown has become an international opinion leader on humanitarian issues like vaccine distribution as well as an influential voice on the future of the UK. Those who have a lowlier position in the political food chain can make an impact, post-retirement, in specialised or local campaigning or charities and community activities. Tony

Benn explained his retirement as due to a wish to **'spend more time on politics'**.

LEGACIES AND EPITAPHS

Politicians, like everyone else, want to be remembered well. And since they have been public figures, they would expect to be remembered well by the public and not just family and friends. They may, however, be remembered best for what they did outside of politics. Michael Foot, a fine writer, was once described as *'a good man fallen among politicians'*.

Few will have the luxury, like Charles de Gaulle and Winston Churchill, of planning their own state funeral in detail. But amongst recently deceased politicians of note, Margaret Thatcher merited a suitably grand service at St Paul's, attended by the royal family and overseas dignitaries. Paddy Ashdown merited a memorial service in Westminster Abbey, Shirley Williams in Westminster Cathedral. John Smith died prematurely and was buried on the Isle of Iona. His modest gravestone, which has become a mecca for his admirers, including me, has the inscription: *'An honest man is the noblest work of God'* (Alexander Pope).

Memories fade and only time will tell if politicians are remembered well or remembered at all. I cannot advise you on death, yet, but I can commend the experience of retiring from politics on a modest political high and young enough, aged 76, to embark on a new career.

Every day the increasing weight of years admonishes me more and more, that the shade of retirement is as necessary to me as it will be welcome.

George Washington, Farewell Address

The bed covers were down, and concealed underneath the bed was a pail, with a tube full of bile coming out of me. I made my resignation to the Queen of England for an hour, in great discomfort.

Harold Macmillan

No man will ever carry out of the presidency the reputation which carried him into it.

Thomas Jefferson

It would have been a very, very good thing if the next election after Margaret went we had lost.
Denis Thatcher

Those who believe that after I have left the government as prime minister, I will go into a permanent retirement, really should have their heads examined.
Lee Kuan Yew

The three ages of man: youth, middle age, and 'You're looking well, Enoch.'
Enoch Powell to Matthew Parris, who had ventured the comment

I am glad to be going. This is the loneliest place in the world.
William Howard Taft to his successor, Woodrow Wilson

Now I will return to my village, and there will remain at the disposition of the nation.
Charles de Gaulle

What other consolation can be sought when one has faced history?
Charles de Gaulle on Colombey-les-deux-Églises

YES, MY LORD

I am dead; dead, but in the Elysian Fields.
Benjamin Disraeli on his arrival in the House of Lords

If like me you are over 90, frail, on two sticks, half dead and half blind, you stick out like a sore thumb in most places, but not in the House of Lords. Besides, they seem to have a bar and a loo within 30 yards in any direction.
Harold Macmillan (Earl of Stockton)

Bye! I won't miss you.

Cherie Blair, to the Downing Street press on leaving

Other people's opinions matter less – unless they're medical.
Baroness Trumpington

The candle in that great turnip has gone out.
Winston Churchill on the retirement of Stanley Baldwin

I am then to be liberated from the hated occupations of politics, & to sink into the bosom of my family, my farm & my books. I have my house to build, my fields to farm, and to watch for the happiness of those who labour for mine.

Thomas Jefferson, 1793. He returned to become president

And still the question, 'What shall be done with our ex-Presidents?' is not laid at rest; and I sometimes think Watterson's solution of it, 'Take them out and shoot them', is worthy of attention.

Grover Cleveland. Watterson was a newspaper editor who believed any former president would be a danger to the nation

There is an old girl called Anno Domini that catches up with us, and she has been trying to catch up with me . . . It just seems to me to make sense to move out of the White House voluntarily without waiting to be carried out.

Harry S Truman

Thank goodness I won't have to go to that bloody thing this year.

Denis Thatcher on the Conservative Party conference, after his wife's overthrow

The only man to move from the Cabinet table to the restaurant table and consider it a promotion.

Norman Fowler on Roy Hattersley

Do you remember when I said that bombing would begin in five minutes? When I fell asleep during the audience with the Pope? Those were the good old days.

Ronald Reagan

She is in danger of becoming the Tony Benn of the Tory party – old and mad and silly and wrong.

Edwina Currie on Lady Thatcher

ACKNOWLEDGEMENTS

I owe a great debt to the many people who helped me, in ways great and small, through 10 general elections, 20 years in Parliament, 5 years in government and 2 years as party leader. Without them there would be no political career for me to write about. Those experiences gave me the raw material to combine with the quotations which were compiled by Nick Comfort.

I am grateful to Drummond Moir for the idea behind the book, for encouragement and critical guidance to write it. He, together with Jessica Patel, carried out the careful editing.

My thanks too to my literary agent Georgina Capel for recommending me for the project and the project to me.

INDEX